The Persistence of Unemployment
Hysteresis in Canadian Labour Markets

The deep recession and slow recovery of the Canadian economy in the 1980s and the lengthy recession of the early 1990s raised serious questions about economic policy making. The steady increase in Canadian unemployment rates led some economists to doubt the traditionally held view that the national economy is by nature self-correcting and to endorse the concept of hysteresis – the idea that the unemployment rate may display no tendency to return to an unchanging natural rate. Such hysteresis would have important and far-reaching implications for economic policy, particularly monetary policy. In *The Persistence of Unemployment*, Stephen Jones presents a comprehensive assessment of persistent unemployment, specifically hysteresis, in Canadian labour markets.

Jones provides an overview of leading theories of hysteresis and examines evidence from Canada and abroad from both microeconomic and macroeconomic perspectives. He extends the econometric analysis of hysteresis at both the micro and macro levels and concludes that while there is some evidence of dependence in Canada, the overall picture is not one of hysteresis.

The Persistence of Unemployment is essential for understanding an important current debate on economic policy making.

STEPHEN R.G. JONES is professor of economics, McMaster University.

The Persistence of Unemployment

Hysteresis in Canadian Labour Markets

STEPHEN R.G. JONES

McGill-Queen's University Press
Montreal & Kingston • London • Buffalo

ISBN 0-7735-1307-8

Legal deposit third quarter 1995
Bibliothèque nationale du Québec

Printed in the United States on acid-free paper

This book has been published with the help of a grant from the Social Science Federation of Canada, using funds provided by the Social Sciences and Humanities Research Council of Canada.

McGill-Queen's University Press is grateful to the Canada Council for support of its publication program.

Canadian Cataloguing in Publication Data

Jones, Stephen R. G.
The persistence of unemployment : hysteresis in Canadian labour markets
Includes bibliographical references and index.
ISBN 0-7735-1307-8
1. Unemployment – Canada. 2. Unemployment (Economic theory). I. Title.
HD5728.J66 1995 331.13'7971 C95-900409-2

Typeset in Times Ten 10.5/13
by Caractéra production graphique, Quebec City

Lines from "My Hometown" by Bruce Springsteen are published by permission of Jon Landau Management.

To Amy and Robin

Contents

Figures and Tables

FIGURES

TABLES

Acknowledgments

This book grew out of work undertaken for the Economic Council of Canada in what turned out to be its final year of existence. I would like to thank many economists formerly at the council for support, encouragement, and criticism during the phases of this research. In particular, Ross Preston was a wise guide who, while probably wishing that the conclusions and my interpretations had turned out somewhat differently, never failed in his strong support of the independence of my work. Also at the council, Miles Corak and Surendra Gera generously provided valuable comments and insights; Miles Corak, now at Statistics Canada, provided extensive comments on an early draft of this manuscript.

I would like to thank all the participants in a seminar at the Economic Council of Canada, especially Garnett Picot of Statistics Canada, for pertinent criticism. At McMaster University, I would like to thank my colleagues, especially Martin Browning, John Burbidge, Alan Harrison, Peter Kuhn, Lonnie Magee, Stuart Mestelman, Bill Scarth, and Mike Veall, for their support, suggestions, and corrections during the period of research. I would also like to thank Bernard Bonin, of the Bank of Canada, and Pierre Fortin, Université du Québec à Montréal, for extensive comments on an early draft of this work. Two anonymous referees provided a range of insightful comments that have improved both the substance and the presentation of the material. McMaster graduate students Arthur Sweetman and Ramesh Subramaniam provided very able research assistance.

Barry Cozier and Gordon Wilkinson of the Bank of Canada and Pierre Fortin of Université du Québec à Montréal gave me access to previously used data in an exemplary spirit of scholarly cooperation. Such access made possible the replication and robustness assessments performed in the text, and I acknowledge with gratitude the assistance of these colleagues. I am grateful as well to Scott Murray and Steve Roller of Statistics Canada, who facilitated access to the unpublished Labour Force Survey data used extensively in the microeconomic estimation and testing.

This book has been published with the help of a grant from the Social Science Federation of Canada, using funds provided by the Social Sciences and Humanities Research Council of Canada. In addition, the Social Sciences and Humanities Research Council of Canada has supported my research on these topics in labour economics, and I am grateful for this support.

Finally, I would like to thank Ellen Badone for her continued help and support.

The Persistence of Unemployment

1 Introduction

> Now Main Street's whitewashed windows and vacant stores
> Seems like there ain't nobody wants to come down here
> no more
> They're closing down the textile mill across the railroad tracks
> Foreman says these jobs are going boys and they ain't
> coming back
>
> Bruce Springsteen, "My Hometown," 1984

The deep recession of the early 1980s and the slow recovery of the Canadian economy through much of the rest of the decade raised a number of serious questions about the role and conduct of economic policy-making. As unemployment rose to levels unseen since the 1930s, growing numbers of people experienced the grim reality of long-term joblessness, exhaustion of eligibility for unemployment insurance benefits, rising debt and dependence on family members or on social assistance, and gradual realization of poor future prospects. Disparities in provincial experience have widened over the past few decades, and, within each region, much of the burden of the higher unemployment has fallen on specific groups – the young, those with less than eight years of schooling and, in increasing proportions in the 1980s, workers aged between 55 and 64.

The recession of the early 1990s, though differing in a number of important respects from that of the 1980s,[1] has underscored the upward trend in the national rate of unemployment – a pattern that has continued almost unabated since 1945. Perhaps most important, this recession has shown that no one is immune from the consequences of economic downturn – not the steelworker in Cape Breton, not the logger in the west, and not the curator at the Art Gallery of Ontario.

CHALLENGING THE ORTHODOXY

Such steady worsening of Canadian unemployment has led some commentators to query the mainstream view of how the economy operates and even to doubt the self-correcting nature of the national economy. The prevailing view through most of the 1950s and 1960s was that there existed in Western economies some sort of trade-off between inflation and unemployment, termed the Phillips curve, after A.W. Phillips, who first noted such a long-run empirical regularity. This phenomenon was seen as presenting a "menu" of policy choices. A high level of economic activity would produce greater inflationary pressure and increase employment, while low inflation could be bought at the cost of underused factories and equipment, plant slowdowns, depressed consumer spending, and higher unemployment.

This understanding of the relationship between unemployment and inflation was seriously undercut, however, in the late 1960s, most famously in Milton Friedman's 1967 presidential address ("The Role of Monetary Policy") to the American Economic Association (Friedman 1968). Friedman presented economic fluctuations as temporary departures from a *natural rate of unemployment*, with upturns and downturns moving the economy relative to some long-run, equilibrium level of unemployment towards which the economy was inevitably drawn. Friedman's words are telling; in his description, this natural rate "is the level that would be ground out by the Walrasian system of general equilibrium equations, provided there is embedded in them the actual structural characteristics of the labour and commodity markets, including market imperfections, stochastic variability in demands and supplies, the cost of gathering information about job vacancies and labour availabilities, the costs of mobility, and so on" (1968, 8).[2] Thus, the natural rate is a long-run equilibrium concept and as such does not exclude the possibility of temporary fluctuations. It incorporates market, informational, and institutional imperfections that affect the production of output and hiring of labour, and it recognizes the structural characteristics of the economy – its industries and their seasonal and cyclical sensitivities, its demographic composition, its position in the world economy and other factors. Most important, according to Friedman's definition, the natural rate could vary through time, if the underlying structural determinants varied.

In the late 1960s, the critical aspect of Friedman's position lay not so much in the dependence of the natural rate on real-world structural features and imperfections as in his related argument that the Phillips curve presented a fallacious view of policy choices. Friedman's argument, which became central to much policy analysis, was that while an economy might exhibit a *statistical* Phillips curve – in that high inflation tended to occur when unemployment was low, and vice versa – such a relationship might not be exploitable by the economic policy-maker. The correlation observed in the data might not truly be causal. Over the longer term, changes in all prices and wages together, as occur with generalized inflation, could be expected to have little effect on the volume of trade, output, and unemployment, since all of these magnitudes ought to respond to real variables – that is, to the ratio of one price to another. To the extent that consumer prices rise in step with an individual's wage, she may end up no better or worse off than before, and her decisions about how much to work may not alter. Or, if a firm's input prices increase in parallel with the price of its output, it similarly may be doing as well as before and may not wish to alter its level of production. Thus, Friedman argued, over the long term at least, there should be little or no relationship between inflation and unemployment: the long-run Phillips curve is vertical.

In the short run, however, according to Friedman, mistakes, misperceptions, and confusion about relative price changes versus general price changes could generate a statistical Phillips curve, which would disappear when such informational imperfections were eliminated and only relative prices were considered. Only in so far as agents happened to be "fooled" – confounding relative and general price changes – could the economy deviate from the natural rate of unemployment. Friedman's original argument was based on a simple model of inflationary expectations that depended on the recent past experience of inflation, from which it followed that, to fool agents and permanently attain unemployment below the natural rate, inflation had to be always accelerating. In essence, the (naïve) adaptive expectations that he envisaged would then never catch up to the actual rate, and such "accelerationist" policy could beat the limits apparently posed by the natural rate of unemployment.

Of course, Friedman's accelerationist conception was a reductio ad absurdum, since permanently accelerating inflation could clearly itself have harmful consequences. This policy prescription was purely a consequence of the particular adaptive-expectations mechanism that Friedman considered; more sophisticated (or "rational") expectations would not be fooled even by the permanently accelerating policy, for example. None the less, this idea that the natural rate might be linked to the change in the rate of inflation has persisted – indeed, one popular interpretation carries the acronym NAIRU – "non-accelerating inflation rate of unemployment." This view of the natural rate has clear empirical content, depending on whether inflation is increasing or slowing, in a way that Friedman's original definition did not. With some modifications, the NAIRU remains the prevailing way of thinking empirically about the natural rate, and it ties in with theory to the extent that changing rates of inflation are driven by differing degrees of tightness within the labour market.[3] The principal alternative is to use a wider range of cyclical indicators – measures of capacity utilization, housing starts, interest rates, and so on – and to construct a cyclically adjusted rate of unemployment.

A RISING NATURAL RATE?

Problems began to emerge with these natural-rate interpretations of economic fluctuations in the late 1970s and early 1980s, in Canada and elsewhere. On various measures, the evidence seemed to indicate a rise in the natural rate. Certainly, many economies had seen an indisputable rise in the actual rate of unemployment; Figure I.1 gives the Canadian and US evidence, together with the historical comparison afforded by pushing the time series back to the 1920s.[4] However, researchers generally had some difficulty in documenting the set of changes in the structural determinants that could have explained this generalized and persistent rise. Moreover, in many countries, especially in Europe, a fairly high and stable rate of inflation occurred simultaneous with persistently high unemployment, suggesting that the NAIRU had risen.

There were three main reactions to these observations. First, some economists preferred to view the growth of unemployment into the 1980s as aberrant and as merely a relatively long-lived departure from equilibrium, just as some argued in the 1970s that the Great Depression was receding into history as one anomaly, rather than as the prime example of a failure of an economy's self-

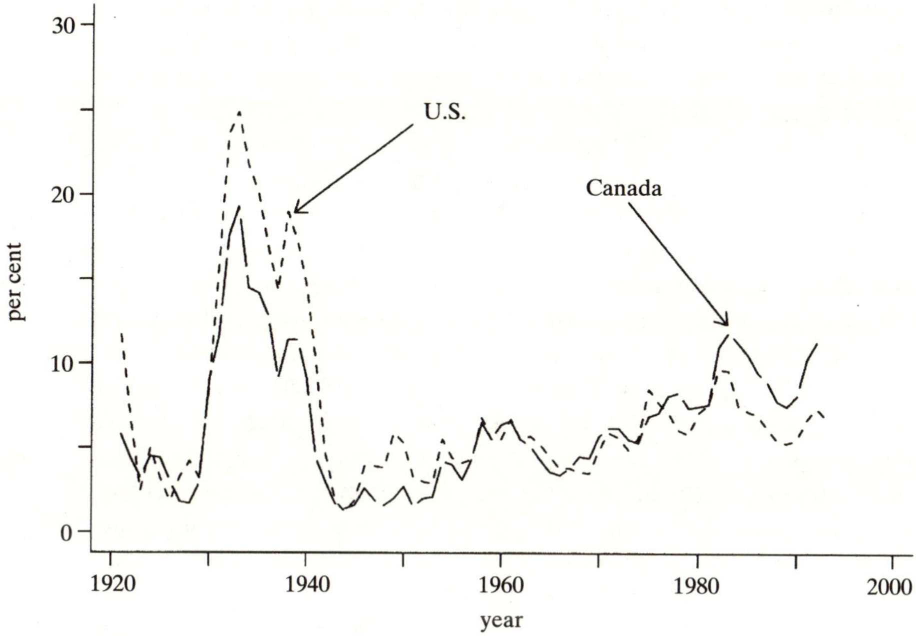

Figure 1.1
Unemployment rates

regulating abilities. A second response sought to document, for each country and each period, the structural factors that had led to the widespread rise in average unemployment rates; examples include growth of female labour-force participation and extension of employment-protection legislation. On this view, as Friedman foresaw, such structural change had indeed moved natural rates, with actual rates being pulled along in their wake.

A third reaction was to conclude that the natural rate did appear to have risen, in many economies and in many periods, but to doubt the explanations based on changing structural conditions. This approach led to re-evaluation of the Friedmanesque orthodoxy of a natural rate depending on (a well-defined set of) observables and to development of the main alternative: that the natural rate, in some way, followed the actual rate.[5] When an adverse shock hits an economy – an oil price rise or a sudden slowing in the growth of the money supply, for example – unemployment rises and pulls up the natural rate. Even when the shock has passed, the natural rate towards which the economy may converge in the long run is now higher than before, and the temporary shock can have a long-lasting, even permanent effect. In essence, then, the unemployment rate is seen as history-dependent, with no necessary tendency to revert to an unchanging natural rate.

This idea is encapsulated in the concept of hysteresis, according to which the history of the economy must be understood in order to explain its current position. The term *hysteresis* was coined by the Scottish physicist-engineer James Alfred Ewing in 1881 to describe transient current generated by twisting magnetic wires – "these curves exhibit, in a striking manner, a persistence of previous state … to this action … the author now gives the name Hysteresis" (Ewing 1881, quoted in Cross and Allan 1988, 26) – and is still common through the hysteresis loop diagram in texts on electromagnetism (see, for example, Cross and Allan 1988, 29). The idea of history-dependence is by no means new in economics. Schumpeter referred to economic dynamics that had hysteresis-like elements (Cross and Hutchinson 1988, 3, for example), while Strotz, Elster, and others have studied habit-formation and dependence in formation of preferences. Even Samuelson, whose equilibrium models typically eschew such effects, colourfully noted that "in our more realistic moods, we tacitly used models involving hysteresis: Spain would never be the same after Columbus; Scarlett O'Hara would be permanently affected by the Confederate inflation … obviously, in such models all real variables do not end up unchanged as a result of certain unbalanced introductions of new M [money] into the system" (Samuelson 1972, 540–1, quoted in Cross and Hutchinson 1988, 3–4).[6]

Applied to labour markets, the concept of hysteresis means that unemployment can drift, pulling the "natural rate" along with it. The history of the economy determines the current natural rate. A downturn raises the current unemployment rate and, through hysteresis, the natural rate from that point on. Such drift in the natural rate leaves no real anchor for the making of economic policy.

In Canada, doubt about the relevance of Friedmanesque natural rate theory grew following the deep recession of 1981–82 and the lethargic recovery, which showed considerable regional diversity. Unemployment stayed high nationally, even as the corresponding US figures declined sharply by mid-decade.[7] This economic performance generated lively debate about whether policy, especially monetary policy, had been and continued to be too restrictive, driving the Canadian economy into a made-at-home recession and failing to allow it to recover in step with the United States. Disputes arose in Canada and elsewhere over the appropriate measurement of the natural rate. Economists found it difficult to pinpoint changes in structural factors that could fully account for the general deterioration in performance.

Some discussion focused on the so-called sacrifice ratio – the amount of unemployment that must be endured (or output lost) for a one-percentage-point drop in the rate of inflation.[8] On the standard natural-rate view, the unemployment or loss of output is considered temporary, with the natural rate of unemployment and the potential level of output acting as long-run anchors, no matter what the temporary shock, while, conversely, the reduction in the rate of inflation is seen as permanent. Thus, economic policy, especially monetary policy, amounts to offsetting short-term and temporary losses against longer-term but permanent gains. Even with reasonable discounting of future gains against present-day losses, so that the permanent gains of lower inflation came at the immediate cost of unemployment, this view left comparatively little room for dispute over the ideal target rate of inflation.[9] Zero, or something close to it, appeared to be the goal and such a target continues to hold sway. As John Crow, then governor of the Bank of Canada, argued a few years ago, "the experience of recent years only confirms the importance of achieving price stability as a basic condition of sustained good overall economic performance" (1988, 17).

The idea of hysteresis has the potential to turn this debate around, however. If labour markets are characterized by hysteresis, the costs of an anti-inflationary policy can turn out to be permanent, not temporary. An increase in the rate of unemployment also raises the "natural" rate to which the actual level will gravitate. With the costs of higher unemployment or lost output being felt immediately and in every period into the future, the cost-benefit analysis of reducing inflation can be dramatically reversed. Clearly, then, it matters greatly for purposes of economic policy whether or not Canadian labour markets are characterized by such hysteresis.[10]

OUTLINE OF THIS STUDY

This book seeks to provide a comprehensive and objective assessment of the importance of hysteresis for the analysis of Canadian labour markets. I begin by surveying the leading theories of hysteresis in chapter 2. Though many such theories have been advanced, some have exhibited greater endurance than others, and, for purposes of empirical assessment, it is critical to assess their various strengths and weaknesses. Also, from the point of view of economic policy-making, these theories differ substantially in their implications. I concentrate on a number of the hypothesized causes of hysteresis, including processes of bargaining, workers' losses of skills in times of recession, employers' biases against the long-term unemployed, underinvestment in the capital stock, and policy-induced causes of hysteresis, such as that resulting from unemployment insurance. Chapter 2 also examines a number of concepts related to hysteresis that have been associated with models of economies characterized by multiple equilibria. In such models, knowledge of all the structural determinants is not sufficient to determine which of many possible equilibria is reached: the economy could get stuck at a poor outcome with high unemployment or could land at a good outcome with low unemployment. Though the dynamic process that might lead an economy from one equilibrium to another is often incompletely specified in such models, these theories do generate a range of insights that complements the work based on hysteresis itself.

I then review the existing empirical evidence on hysteresis, first internationally and then with a close look at work on the Canadian economy. Chapter 3 surveys the international evidence, primarily for the United States, Europe, and Japan. This evidence is of five main types. First, there are statistical studies of single economic variables, such as a measure of national income or the rate of unemployment, that seek to determine whether these variables individually appear to remain constant around some level. For unemployment, the level around which the unemployment rate might remain constant would be interpreted as the natural rate, of course. Second, I look at studies involving the relationships among a number of variables, such as the Phillips curve relationship between inflation and unemployment, and assess whether allowance should be made for hysteresis in these formulations. Third, I look at a number of microeconomic-based studies that use data at the level of the individual, rather than data for the economy as a whole. This approach is motivated largely by the theoretical work on bargaining processes in chapter 2. Fourth, I give some consideration to a small literature that tries to test for multiplicity of equilibria, using US and British data. Finally, I assess research on long-term unemployment and the idea of duration dependence in unemployment – when prospects of finding work vary with elapsed duration of the unemployment spell. One example would occur if, as an individual's unemployment spell lengthens, her job prospects steadily worsen. This idea ties in with theories of potential skill loss and with the view that employers might have a bias against the longer-term unemployed.

The empirical evidence for Canada surveyed in chapter 4 tends to follow similar lines to the findings in other nations, though with some distinctive features. I first look at recent macroeconomic results on the Canadian Phillips curve. This research turns out to be somewhat conflicting in its conclusions, a point to which I return in subsequent chapters. Related to this work are estimates of a natural rate of unemployment for Canada, and I next review the wide range of results on the natural rate that various methods have produced. Also, I examine research on the operation of the Canadian unemployment insurance system, with special reference to regionally extended benefits. Such benefits have the potential to induce hysteresis, with the generosity of the system expanding as (regional) unemployment rates rise, and with such generosity potentially inducing a further increase in unemployment. Whether such potential feedback is realized, however, is less than clear, and I analyse the argument in some detail. Finally, I look at Canadian long-term unemployment and the microeconomic analysis of duration dependence. Though still fairly low relative to many European countries, domestic long-term unemployment rose markedly in the 1980s, and there are some signs that duration-dependence may be important even for quite short spells of unemployment. Overall, the existing Canadian evidence on hysteresis is patchy, with some areas being relatively ignored while others have been explored at length. Thus this evidence does not present a conclusive and consistent argument either for or against the existence of hysteresis in the Canadian economy.

The remainder of the book presents a comprehensive appraisal of the evidence on hysteresis in Canadian labour markets, remedying the evident omissions and deficiencies in the existing literature. This appraisal is based on several new research projects, some of which use recent, major data sources not available for past work.

I first address the macroeconomic findings in chapter 5, looking both at the properties of Canadian unemployment rates and at the robustness of a number of alternative methods of testing for hysteresis in a Phillips curve context. This analysis of robustness – the sensitivity of the results to small and apparently insignificant changes in model specification – resolves the apparent inconsistencies in earlier work.

The microeconomic analysis is presented in chapter 6, where I use two individual-level sources of data from the 1980s to study the potential for various types of duration and state dependence in jobless spells. Two recent and informative data sources provide the bulk of the evidence. First, the 1986–87 Labour Market Activity Survey (LMAS), a large and representative sample of households in the ten provinces, is employed. The LMAS was administered as a supplement to the Labour Force Survey (LFS), the basic survey from which the unemployment rate is calculated. Unlike the LFS, however, which covers an individual for only a maximum of six consecutive months, the LMAS provides evidence on periods of employment and non-employment over a continuous two-year period, together with key supplementary information on an individual's demographics and region. Most of my analysis is based on a sample of over 21,000 jobless spells, using only the first such spell any individual experienced in the two years covered by the LMAS. One issue that arises in this work is the congruence between jobless spells from the LMAS and unemployment spells, as would enter into the usual LFS definition of the unemployment rate.[11] Differences between joblessness and unemployment will naturally arise whenever individuals move out of the labour force for reasons such as education, discouragement, family arrangements, and retirement. It is clearly important to separate these types of non-employment spells from unemployment as usually measured.

To address this issue, the second dataset, which is unique to this research project, uses a special, individual-level matching of the LMAS and the contemporaneous unemployment information collected in the LFS itself. Thus the unemployment spells recorded in this dataset correspond exactly to the measure of unemployment used in the national unemployment rate. These new data, termed the LMAS-LFS dataset, provide evidence on nearly 7,000 unemployment spells of varying length in 1986–87, linked to all of the information furnished by the LMAS itself.

Using both sources, I analyse a number of models that estimate the probability that a spell (of joblessness or of unemployment, respectively) ends in a given period, allowing this probability to vary as a spell progresses. Such models, termed hazard models,[12] are the natural way to investigate the potential for duration dependence that constitutes a primary microeconomic foundation for economy-wide hysteresis. In all cases, the hazards are estimated conditional on the other information available about the individual in a spell of joblessness or unemployment. The analysis looks at two particular variants of these hazard models: one that imposes some special structure, restricting the hazard to following one of several families of pre-specified shapes; and one that places little structure on the nature of the duration dependence and therefore allows any pattern of changing hazards as a spell progresses. The latter class of models, for example, would allow the probability of moving into employment to fall sharply at the start of a spell, to remain fairly constant from 1 to 6 months, to rise around the time of likely exhaustion of eligibility for unemployment insurance benefits, and to decline steadily in the months of long-term joblessness following such exhaustion.

The final section of chapter 6 looks at the estimation of a labour-market "matching function" based on Canadian data. The idea here is to study the relationship between the inputs that generate matches between workers and employers – the number of unemployed, the number of reported vacancies – and the outputs of such matching, measured as the number of individuals flowing into employment in each month. From the theoretical work in chapter 2, it is clear that the properties of such a matching function are critical in determining the potential for multiple equilibria. I present a set of estimates that permit us to assess this potential for the Canadian economy.

Overall, what results do all of these research avenues yield? Somewhat to my surprise, the Canadian evidence seems to lead to relatively clear-cut conclusions. The macroeconomic work provides little evidence of hysteresis, with the few indications in favour of hysteresis being fragile results that are not "robust" to very minor changes in statistical or economic specification. The evidence for hysteresis from the microeconomic work is slightly more mixed, with some signs of state dependence in unemployment and jobless spells. However, the degree of such dependence and the numbers of people involved at the longer durations are never sufficient to generate substantial hysteresis in the economy as a whole. Moreover, since the microeconomic work operates from the viewpoint of one individual, it may of course be offset at the level of the overall economy, so that there is no necessary link between the macroeconomic and microeconomic results. That is, while there is some evidence of dependence in the microeconomic spells, the summary picture is not one of hysteresis.

Should I have been surprised by these results? With hindsight, perhaps they should not have been unexpected. When Bruce Springsteen wrote of the declining textile mills of New Jersey, the unemployment rate in that state had peaked at 9.0 per cent in 1982. By 1988, New Jersey's unemployment rate was down to 3.8 per cent, a level so low that an innovative unemployment insurance experimental program ran into difficulties owing to lack of recruits. Though the textile jobs may have gone for ever, the state's economy seemed to be at full employment by the later part of the decade. Other jobs had evidently taken their place. Of course, it is important not to understate the real problems of transition that may occur in such a process of change. But this type of transitional difficulty does not amount to hysteresis.

2 Theories of Hysteresis and Multiple Equilibria

This chapter surveys theories of hysteresis, with primary attention being given to labour markets, and discusses related concepts associated with models of multiple equilibria. From the outset, it should be recognized that, beyond testing whether or not the concept applied to a particular economy, a key issue is the cause of such extreme persistence. Many structural factors can generate hysteresis, and, for some empirical assessment and policy analysis, it can matter which model or models apply in a given circumstance.

In this chapter, I address models related to insider-outsider bargaining, other models of union membership dynamics, models of "de-skilling" and the loss of human capital in recessions, models where underinvestment in physical capital is the key, and models that suggest increased persistence (though not necessarily hysteresis) as a result of specific aspects of the unemployment insurance system. I also cover market-based models of multiple macroeconomic equilibria, especially those related to labour markets through the processes of job search and matching worker and employer. Market-based causes of unemployment persistence or hysteresis are important in such a framework, and alternative theories of wage determination may be the key to understanding when such multiple equilibria can arise. Consideration is also given to models with a range of potential values for a "natural rate" of unemployment, as developed in recent work on economies with imperfect competition in product and/or labour markets.

THEORIES OF HYSTERESIS

Insider-Outsider Models

Insider-outsider models of wage determination have come to comprise the leading variant in the microeconomic modelling of hysteresis and will accordingly be examined at somewhat greater length than the other theories that generate hysteresis. Developed variously by Gregory (1986), Blanchard and Summers (1986), and Lindbeck and Snower (1988), this approach presents wages as being set by some sort of bargaining process between a firm and its existing labour force – the "insiders" – with little apparent representation of others – "outsiders" – typically taken as the unemployed.[1] In the simplest case, the traditional monopoly model of union behaviour is modified so that, while the workers (perhaps through a union) unilaterally select a real wage and the firm then selects the employment level, given this wage, in the first stage the wage is set so as to keep the existing workforce employed. With uncertain demand for the product and hence for labour by the firm, and in the absence of contingent wage-setting, such a wage might be achieved on average, or, if allowance is made for some aversion to layoff risk, workers may select a wage so that expected employment is somewhat greater than membership (e.g. Blanchard and Summers 1986; Katz 1988).[2]

To see the stark implications of this type of model, let labour demand be given by

$$n = \mathrm{a} - \mathrm{b}w + e, \tag{2.1}$$

where n and w are the logarithms of employment and the real wage, respectively, a and b are positive constants, and e is a mean-zero-error term reflecting shocks to labour demand after the wage has been determined. Dynamic aspects of labour demand are ignored for the sake of simplicity. If those employed at the time of wage-setting are identified as the current union membership, denoted by m, then for the wage to secure full employment of this membership level, on average, it follows that

$$m = En = \mathrm{a} - \mathrm{b}w, \tag{2.2}$$

where En is the expected value of n. Accordingly, employment is equal to membership plus a mean-zero-error term:

$$n = m + e. \tag{2.3}$$

Finally, since membership is here given by the existing labour force, the result is that

$$n = n_{-1} + e, \tag{2.4}$$

where n_{-1} denotes the lagged value of employment (i.e. the employment level in the preceding period when wages were set). Thus the conclusion from this simple model is that employment follows a random walk.

Such a model, though useful in focusing attention on the idea of insiders' power, has a number of major problems. First, it is explicitly *not* a model derived from the individual, optimizing decisions of agents (see, for example, Kennan's 1986 comment on Blanchard and Summers), and the failure to allow for contingent wage settlements is potentially crucial. Work that has paid greater attention to such concerns (e.g. Drazen and Gottfries 1987; Gottfries and Horn 1987; Roberts 1989; and Ellis and Holden 1991) blunts these sharp conclusions. Second, with a given labour force, it follows from (2.4) that, if employment obeys a random walk, then so does unemployment. With natural boundaries at zero and the size of the labour force that will eventually be reached with probability one, the long-run implications of an exact random walk are not reasonable. Furthermore, modification of the wage-setting goal to allow for workers' perceptions of layoff risk would naturally tend to exacerbate this odd result, since employment would now follow a random walk with positive drift, eliminating unemployment in the long run. Third, since most countries' labour forces have grown over time, simple application of (2.4) would imply that such increases should have been reflected largely in a growth of unemployment; this does not square with the facts.

The simple insider-outsider model posits no link whatsoever between wage-setting and the state of the economy, as measured by unemployment. A more sensible model would allow such connection, probably though two mechanisms. First, the level of unemployment should affect the bargaining positions adopted by incumbent workers, since it indicates such a worker's likely ease or difficulty in obtaining another job. To the extent that there is aversion to layoff risk, it is reasonable that such aversion be greater when economic times are bad and prospects poor than in booms. Second, a reasonable analysis will also allow for some responsiveness by firms. If the extreme monopoly model is dropped and one allows a firm some bargaining power over the wage, while still letting it retain the right to set employment (the so-called right to manage), then the level of unemployment should also affect its ability to resist the bargaining demands of the union through the option to hire from the ranks of the unemployed.

A simple model that permits a role for the level of unemployment is sketched by Blanchard (1991). Static labour demand is given by

$$n = -w + \varepsilon, \tag{2.5}$$

and firms are still assumed to set employment, given the wage w and the disturbance term ε; all variables are in logarithms. Let w^* denote the wage that will keep employment unchanged on average, so that

$$w^* = -n_{-1}. \tag{2.6}$$

In addition, let w_r denote the reservation wage of the workers – the minimum level at which workers will choose to supply their labour – and let n_r denote average employment level corresponding to this reservation wage, so that

$$n_r = -w_r. \tag{2.7}$$

Denote the "unemployment rate" as

$$u \equiv n_r - n. \tag{2.8}$$

Blanchard's definition of unemployment here as the shortfall of employment from the level that would be induced by the workers' reservation wage is unusual but convenient, and it turns out that nothing hinges on it. Finally, suppose that wage-setting behaviour reflects bargaining between the union and the firm that can be summarized by

$$w = aw^* + (1 - a)w_r - bEn, \tag{2.9}$$

where the "bargaining power" weight, a, lies between zero and one, and b, the coefficient on expected unemployment (i.e. $n_r - En$), is positive. If we use the wage-setting behaviour of (2.9) in the labour demand curve (2.5), the result follows that

$$u = a/(1 + b)\, u_{-1} - \varepsilon. \tag{2.10}$$

Hence unemployment still follows a first-order, autoregressive process, as in the simplest model (2.4) above, but now the coefficient is equal to $a/(1 + b)$, not unity. In the special case where $a = 1$ and $b = 0$, so that neither the workers' reservation wage nor expected unemployment affects wage determination, the early random walk result is recovered, and the model displays hysteresis. Otherwise, $a/(1 + b)$ lies strictly between zero and one, a case of persistence but not hysteresis. Though this result is important for dynamics, the bottom line in the absence of hysteresis is that the economy must eventually return to the original equilibrium.

Finally, one way to strengthen persistence, without necessarily producing hysteresis, is to examine duration effects. This idea, developed by Layard and Nickell (1987), is that, for whatever reason, the influence of the unemployed on wage-setting behaviour varies inversely with the duration of unemployment.[3] I return below to some of the potential reasons for this effect, together with evidence for and against; here I simply focus on its implications for Blanchard's model. Hence I modify (2.9) to be

$$w = aw^* + (1 - a)w_r - b(\mathrm{E}u - cu_{-1}), \tag{2.11}$$

where c is a constant lying between zero and one; allowing for an nth-order lag polynomial in the unemployment rate produces qualitatively similar results. The central idea behind (2.11) is that, while the short-run effect of unemployment on wage-setting is given by

$-b$, its longer-term effect for n periods is only $-b(1 - c)$; in the limiting case, where $c = 1$, the effect eventually vanishes. Using (2.11) in the static–labour-demand model, I obtain

$$u = a/(1 + b)\, u_{-1} + bc/(1 + b)\, u_{-1} - \varepsilon, \qquad (2.12)$$

so that, relative to (2.10), the second term in (2.12) implies greater persistence in unemployment, as a consequence of the reduced influence on wage-setting of longer-duration unemployment. However, as with the earlier model, (2.12) implies hysteresis only under rather special conditions – namely, that $a = 1$ and $c = 1$. Since neither condition is likely, the result in the basic model of (2.4) does seem extreme and rather unrealistic.[4] That is, while the extreme version of the insider-outsider model gave rise to hysteresis, a reasonable modification of that model induces only persistence, affecting the dynamic path but not the long-run equilibrium of the economy.[5]

Further Theories Based on Union Membership Dynamics

There are a number of other significant papers in the literature that build on union membership effects, analogous to the work of Blanchard and Summers and the pure insider-outsider models. Gottfries and Horn (1987) extend the basic union model with nominal wage-setting prior to realization of a demand shock, allowing explicitly for optimizing behaviour in an intertemporal setting. With two periods, and with layoffs determined by random draw,[6] they show that a union's objective in the second period will be affected by the level of hiring in the first, which has one salient and novel effect. The cost of a wage increase in the second period tends to be reduced, since the likelihood that employed workers will be laid off then is less, the smaller the labour force inherited from the preceding round. The resulting higher wage leads to lower expected employment in the current period, so that temporary shocks can accordingly generate persistent employment effects.

Gottfries and Horn also demonstrate that such results continue to hold in a simple macroeconomic version of the theory. Several qualifications can be made to the basic model. First, the result is typically not hysteresis, but rather persistence, removing the clear-cut result in the ad hoc model of Blanchard and Summers. Second, the two-period nature of the model clearly is in need of some generalization. Third, the firm/industry's demand for labour is assumed to be a function only of the current wage rate. It may, however, depend on current and expected future real wages, as would, for example, be the case in a dynamic setting that incorporates costs of adjustment for employment.

Drazen and Gottfries (1987) build a multi-period, dynamic, optimizing model to address these insider-outsider issues. They demonstrate that, when insiders have priority in hiring and the main influence on wage negotiations, the optimal wage demand rises as the number of workers with seniority declines; hence the model yields persistence of potentially low employment. In addition, their infinite-horizon framework allows consideration of the nature of seniority arrangements and their effect on persistence of employment. They examine temporary layoffs, the length of the probationary period prior to acquisition of seniority, the effect of seniority on preferential hiring, and the degree to which senior and junior workers affect wage demand. It is found that these factors affect both the level of employment and, significantly, its stochastic dynamics.

Roberts (1989) also examines union membership arrangements and their implications for employment patterns. It explicitly studies the feedback whereby union decisions affect membership and union membership affects members' behaviour. In a voting-theoretic model with rational union members, Roberts shows that one of two regimes can obtain – flexible and rigid. In the former, the union's behaviour appears to be indifferent to unemployment, while in the latter, the union wishes to maintain a fixed size, which results in labour hoarding in a slump. In the latter regime, employment changes are lumpy, and small shocks can produce large changes that are not necessarily reversed when the shock itself is – that is, the model displays hysteresis. In a macroeconomic context, the properties of Roberts's model depend naturally on the proportions of firms and unions in each of the two regimes, with the interesting case occurring when a significant number are rigid. If the critical values that give rise to lumpy employment changes are spread out across unions, then the aggregate behaviour will typically be continuous, not discrete, and it will display a complex lag. Thus the model can generate time paths of aggregate employment that depend on a number of recent values and hence could mimic business-cycle behaviour, even though the stochastic specification underlying the model is Markovian.

Some qualification to the type of result found in many of these papers comes from Jones (1987), however, who examines the dynamic properties of a simple, union-firm bargaining model. When contracts lies on the demand curve for labour,[7] and when membership is driven primarily by the path of actual employment – employed workers join the union, and those unemployed leave – it is shown that a dynamic union that cares about its level of membership will select a level of employment that is higher than it would have selected, in the absence of such considerations. Though such work does not address the changing composition of union membership – as would arise in, for example, an overlapping-generations framework – it does suggest that a union's concern with its future membership level may mitigate the sharp results on wages from basic insider-outsider theory.

Three other papers employ related models. Bliss (1990) shows that the natural rate of unemployment that obtains in an economy with trade unions will differ, depending on whether bargaining is conducted in real or in nominal terms, even in the absence of money illusion and other nominal rigidities. However, his model does not explicitly address membership dynamics and does not generate any hysteretic tendency for moving or multiple natural rates.

In contrast, Ellis and Holden (1991) explore the consequences of seniority-based wages.[8] In their overlapping-generations model, wages may rise more quickly than productivity, in part as insurance against uncertain productivity of agents when they are old, and this behaviour of wages can generate differential response by firms to small and large shocks. For small downward movements in product demand, the result is temporary unemployment among younger workers. However, for large negative shocks that threaten to bankrupt the firm, the implicit employment contract is broken, and older, "overpaid" workers are laid off. Following a small shock, young workers are rehired; after a large shock, older workers are not rehired, which gives rise to hysteresis in employment. Ellis and Holden further demonstrate that the extent of this hysteresis depends on the exact specification of the model,[9] though their result is maintained in all the versions that they consider.

Finally, Manning (1993) addresses wage and employment determination in a dynamic model where some (non-union) strike-breakers continue to work during a dispute and where the inside option of the employer in one period is explicitly determined from the employment level realized in the preceding period. The main results are that employment is not necessarily a declining function of the union's bargaining strength and that wages and union density (defined as proportion of employees not working during a strike) are not monotonically related. Though the model is rather particular in its assumptions, so that its results are best considered suggestive only in the context of a broader range of bargaining strategies, Manning's results cast doubt on the basic insider-outsider story, which implies that harassment by incumbents necessarily raises wages and lowers employment.

Underinvestment in Physical Capital

Another theory about hysteresis is based on underinvestment in physical capital. The argument is that recessions can reduce accumulation of physical capital and therefore increase the equilibrium level of unemployment. This argument can be made in a competitive model (e.g. Bruno and Sachs 1985) or in a variety of imperfectly competitive situations (e.g. Malinvaud 1986; Sneessens and Drèze 1986). Blanchard (1990) provides a useful overview of this literature, both theoretical and empirical.

In this type of framework, each monopolistically competitive firm has a target capital stock determined by factor prices and its perception of aggregate demand, and, given an appropriate specification of adjustment costs, an investment equation follows. Consider a simple example, where firms must incur a fixed (capital) cost but where, given this, the only marginal cost of production is from labour and is constant. Free entry and exit of firms will adjust the size of demand that each operating firm faces so as to achieve zero economic profit (inclusive of the capital costs). In this environment, a fall in aggregate demand will lead some firms to close down and hence to a decline in employment and in capital.[10] To the extent that entry is inhibited when demand recovers, such a temporary decline can be associated with a prolonged departure from the initial equilibrium.[11]

There are two major objections levelled at this theory. First, as an empirical matter, the performance of the US economy in the early years of the Second World War suggests that the decline of about 15 per cent in the capital stock between 1929 and 1939 was no real barrier to output growth, given sufficient demand (see, for example, Gordon 1988, 292; and Blanchard 1990, 86). This historical counter-example is especially important because the rapid decline in unemployment between 1939 and 1941 was the result largely of growth of civilian employment. Second, and perhaps more fundamental, the theory is necessarily only partial, since it must beg the question of why an appropriate response in wage-setting behaviour is not forthcoming. Though capital shortage and the closing of firms can obviously play a role, raising the level of unemployment associated with a given level of wage demands, it is not clear why such demands should be taken as given in the face of high unemployment.

De-skilling and Loss of Human Capital

An alternative route whereby temporary increases in unemployment translate into permanent effects comes from the effects on workers themselves through de-skilling and the loss of human capital. Starting at least as early as the work of Phelps (1972) and Tobin (1980), and passing through the growth-theoretic work of Drazen (1979) and to empirical findings of a permanent effect of US recessions on labour productivity (Dickens 1982), these ideas have been given explicit theoretical treatment by Drazen (1985a, 1985b).[12]

In Drazen (1985b), training and acquisition of human capital are reduced by a recession.[13] The model studied has only firm-specific training, which may underestimate the negative long-term effect of recessions, and concentrates on the employment/participation choice,[14] but it highlights the mechanisms involved in any broader picture. In a dynamic model, where the endogenous variables are the stock of skilled labour and the profits of a firm, a transitory shock that affects the value of a firm's output moves the economy away from the unique steady state and, significantly, can depress output after the shock has passed because of its effect on the stock of skilled labour.[15]

More generally, the types of mechanisms that Drazen examines can also have an influence on less tangible factors that none the less affect an individual's marginal product, at least as perceived by an employer.[16] The ability to show up for work on time may be lacking for a young person who has never held a job, for example. Patterns of responsibility and performance suitable for marginal jobs – "bad jobs," in the terminology of the Economic Council of Canada (1990) – may be quite poor training for primary-sector employment. This idea echoes the early institutional literature on dual labour markets (e.g. Doeringer and Piore 1971), as well as some recent work inspired by these types of ideas (e.g. McDonald and Solow 1985).[17]

Finally, as with the capital-shortage models, a model based on a decline in an unemployed worker's marginal productivity (owing to skill loss, say) will generate persistence or hysteresis in unemployment only if it is not accompanied by an appropriate response in wage-setting behaviour.[18]

Other Effects of Unemployment Duration

Further mechanisms operate through unemployment duration to produce hysteresis-type effects, as alluded to above in the discussion of extensions of the insider-outsider framework. One basic idea in this literature is that, whether or not de-skilling and human capital loss are quantitatively important, if employment practices favour people with shorter unemployment duration to those with long duration, other things being equal, then, such policies can lead to persistent effects from temporary employment disruptions.[19] Empirical suggestion that such forces may be significant in Britain, for example, is contained in Layard and Nickell (1987) and Layard and Bean (1989).

A leading case of this idea has been exposited by Blanchard and Diamond (1994), where the idea of ranking – so that firms weakly prefer those with shorter spells out of work – is shown to be potentially important. Ranking, in this theory, reduces the fear of unemployment among current employees, simply because such people would have very short periods of unemployment, were they to be laid off, and consequently higher probability of re-employment than the average member of the current unemployed. Moreover, the longer high unemployment persists, the stronger this effect will become, as those currently unemployed become even less attractive to employers. This theory may explain the apparent insensitivity of wage determination in many European economies to the presence of a large pool of long-term unemployed. Such an argument may hence relate to the observed degree of unemployment persistence in the 1980s.

Pissarides (1992) further illuminates the link between the duration and the persistence of unemployment.[20] Assuming that the long-term unemployed are less profitable hires than the short-term, he shows that, even with constant returns to scale technologies in both matching and production, the implied difference equation in the matching probability of the unemployed is non-linear. This finding can generate a multiplicity of equilibria, more than one of which may be stable and may lead to employment persistence that lasts longer than the maximum duration of unemployment. Finally, Pissarides notes that many natural extensions of his model – for example, when wages depend on firms' and workers' outside options or when discount rates are finite – further complicate the dynamics of employment and unemployment, making multiplicity and instability of equilibria more likely.[21] In subsequent work (Pissarides, n.d.), the theory has been extended to cover different job durations, and Pissarides has shown some simulation results with short jobs and skill loss during unemployment that quite closely mimic British data.

Effects of Unemployment Insurance

A final mechanism that may induce hysteresis in some contexts is the unemployment insurance (UI) system. The basic argument here is that such protection, by subsidizing a period of job search, may somehow raise the duration of unemployment spells and hence aggregate unemployment.[22] Of course, this factor alone does not provide the type of feedback mechanism necessary for hysteresis to develop, since there is no link from higher unemployment to the generosity of the UI system itself. Such a secondary link can be made in two ways.

First, it can be argued that UI can lead an individual to adjust to a life of unemployment, so that intensity of search and related indices may decline with the length of a jobless spell; this leads to duration effects of the type outlined above. Second, the feedback from the unemployment rate to UI can come directly through policies enacted in economic downturns to give greater relief to the victims of the recession.[23] A Canadian variant on this idea emphasizes the role of automatic increases in UI in response to worsening economic conditions, studying the role of (national or regional) extended benefits. Milbourne, Purvis, and Scoones (1991) have addressed the contribution of Canada's regionally based extended benefit program to national unemployment rates in the 1980s along these lines, and I evaluate their argument when I consider Canadian evidence in chapter 4.

MODELS WITH MULTIPLE EQUILIBRIA

In addition to examining models that have given rise to persistence or hysteresis of employment or unemployment, it is important for us to consider a number of mechanisms that generate multiple equilibria. The principal difference between the two sets of literature is that the work on multiplicity has by and large played down both the dynamics of movement from one equilibrium to another and the question of how the economy "selects" one equilibrium over another.[24] But the similarity between the two sets of literature is striking. In that on multiplicity, a temporary shock may dislodge the economy from one equilibrium and to move it to another, with no tendency for a return once the shock has dissipated.[25] Such a move would correspond to hysteresis, of course, and thus such models are useful, even if their dynamics and empirical implications remain incompletely specified.[26] I briefly survey four types of theories that yield multiple equilibria: those based in labour-market processes of search and job-matching; those using the overlapping-generations models standard in much contemporary macroeconomics; those based on imperfectly competitive markets; and some other recent models of non-ergodic economic growth that study problems of coordination in an explicitly stochastic framework.[27]

Search and Matching Models in Labour Markets

Equilibrium theories of search and matching, in labour markets and elsewhere, often display more than one equilibrium. In a valuable exposition of the variety of results in the literature, Mortensen (1989) analyses exactly what features of a model produce multiplicity and shows the interrelationship between the search-matching models and the theories of wage determination addressed above.

His work is closely related to the search-theoretic work of Diamond (1982), Howitt (1988), Howitt and McAfee (1987), and Pissarides (1990), but it also considers insider-outsider models and other analyses of wage-setting. This brief section outlines the principal results from Mortensen's paper.

The central idea in the literature on matching is that there exists a matching technology, written $m(u,v)$, that determines the number of matches, m, reached when there are u unemployed searching workers and v vacant jobs that employers are seeking to fill. It is assumed that the number of matches is increasing in both u and v, that both "inputs" are essential, that average returns m/u and m/v decline in u and v, respectively, and that the matching technology is homogeneous of degree k, so that

$$m(u,v) = u^k \, m(1, v/u). \tag{2.13}$$

These technology restrictions do not rule out the interesting case of increasing returns in matching.

The remainder of the model specifies the expected present value of a job (J) and a vacancy (V), in terms of a firm's profits, and the expected present value of employment (W) and unemployment (U), from a worker's perspective. The model is set in continuous time, and each valuation obeys an "asset-pricing equation" whereby the interest rate multiplied by the valuation must equal the instantaneous "dividend" plus the "expected capital gain" contingent on a change of status. The solution of the model determines these valuations simultaneously. If it is assumed that entry of potential firms acts to keep the expected value of a vacant job at zero, then all that is required to close such a model is a specification of wage-setting behaviour. Three cases are considered.

First, following the well-known solution of Diamond (1971), employers may post wage offers and have workers search sequentially and without recall. In this case, the unemployed optimally follow a reservation-wage property – accepting the first wage offer above the reservation level – and, given the behaviour of other (identical) employers, each firm selects its own wage offer to maximize its expected wealth. This situation inevitably leads to the monopoly solution, where the wage is the lowest offer acceptable to workers and hence equals each worker's reservation wage. This reservation value is determined, given common offers at all firms, by the value of leisure, denoted b, so that this "competitive" solution is just $w = b$. The expected present value of unemployment must then equal the valuation of a job on these terms, so that $W = U$ as well.

Second, a model of wage determination is possible along efficiency-wage lines, such as the shirking model developed by Shapiro and Stiglitz (1984). Here, when a worker may shirk (and hence collect both the wage w and the value of leisure b), and where a firm can monitor workers only with frequency λ, the wage must exceed the value of leisure so as to guarantee that the expected cost of shirking, $\lambda(W - U)$, is at least equal to the immediate gain, b.[28] Hence, in this efficiency-wage equilibrium, $W - U = b/\lambda$, so that there is involuntary unemployment, in the sense that an unemployed worker will envy an otherwise identical employed worker. Also, the extent of the gap between the equilibrium wage and the value of leisure is increasing in the rate at which a typical unemployed worker makes the transition to employment – $m(u,v)/u$.

Third, Mortensen considers the insider-outsider model, which also addresses the possibility of wages exceeding the market-clearing level. Existing employees have some bargaining power, since turnover is costly, so the wage will share the rent that jointly accrues to worker and firm in the event of a successful match. With this total rent being given by $(J - V) + (W - U)$, if the insiders bargain for a share θ, the implied wage will exceed the value of leisure by a positive amount that is increasing in the ratio of vacancies to unemployment.

Given any of these specifications of wage determination, the overall equilibrium of the matching model is found where employment and the value to the firm of an additional worker hired are unchanging through time. When there are diminishing returns in production, Mortensen demonstrates that in each wage-setting case there is a unique natural rate and a unique saddle-path stable steady-state equilibrium. No matter what the wage process, the condition for employment e to be constant amounts to

$$(l - e)\,\eta(J, e) = \delta e, \qquad (2.14)$$

where l is the fixed total pool of workers, δ the discount rate, and $\eta(J, e)$ the hiring frequency per unemployed worker. This locus slopes upward in (e, J) space, since a greater expected value of profitability per worker, J, is needed to maintain a higher level of employment as an equilibrium. The other condition required for steady state is that this valuation of a new hire, J, be constant through time, which entails satisfaction of

$$(r + \delta)\, J = \pi(J, e), \tag{2.15}$$

where $\pi(J, e)$ denotes the profit function. This will be different for each of the three models. In each one, however, it can be shown that the implied stationary locus for J slopes downward, so that there is a unique steady-state value. Moreover, the dynamics are such that this steady state exhibits saddle-path stability; see Figure 2.1. For a given initial value of employment, the expected profitability of a new hire, J, must adjust so as to put the economy on the unique convergent path to this steady state.

These results are overturned, however, if the production process displays increasing returns to scale. In this situation, while the stationary locus for employment continues to slope upward, the set of (e, J) pairs for which the valuation of a vacancy is constant now does the same; this holds qualitatively for each of the three wage-determination mechanisms considered. Moreover, under straightforward regularity conditions, such an economy will have an odd number of multiple equilibria or a continuum of steady-state solutions.

Consider the simplest such case, with three equilibria (Figure 2.2). The top and bottom solutions are both saddle-path stable; given an initial value for employment, optimism can lead to a rational-expectations convergence on the upper saddle-path, while pessimism can lead to similar convergence at the low-level equilibrium. In addition, Mortensen (1991) later found equilibrium-limit cycles around the middle equilibrium. The intuition behind these types of effects is simply that, if the value of a match rises, this raises firms' demand for labour, which creates jobs; in turn, reduced unemployment operates through the thin-market externality to raise the value of a match, confirming the virtuous circle and producing multiplicity and the potential for cycles.[29]

The uniqueness results obtained for diminishing returns are also sometimes lost when there are increasing returns to scale in the matching technology, even if the production technology has only

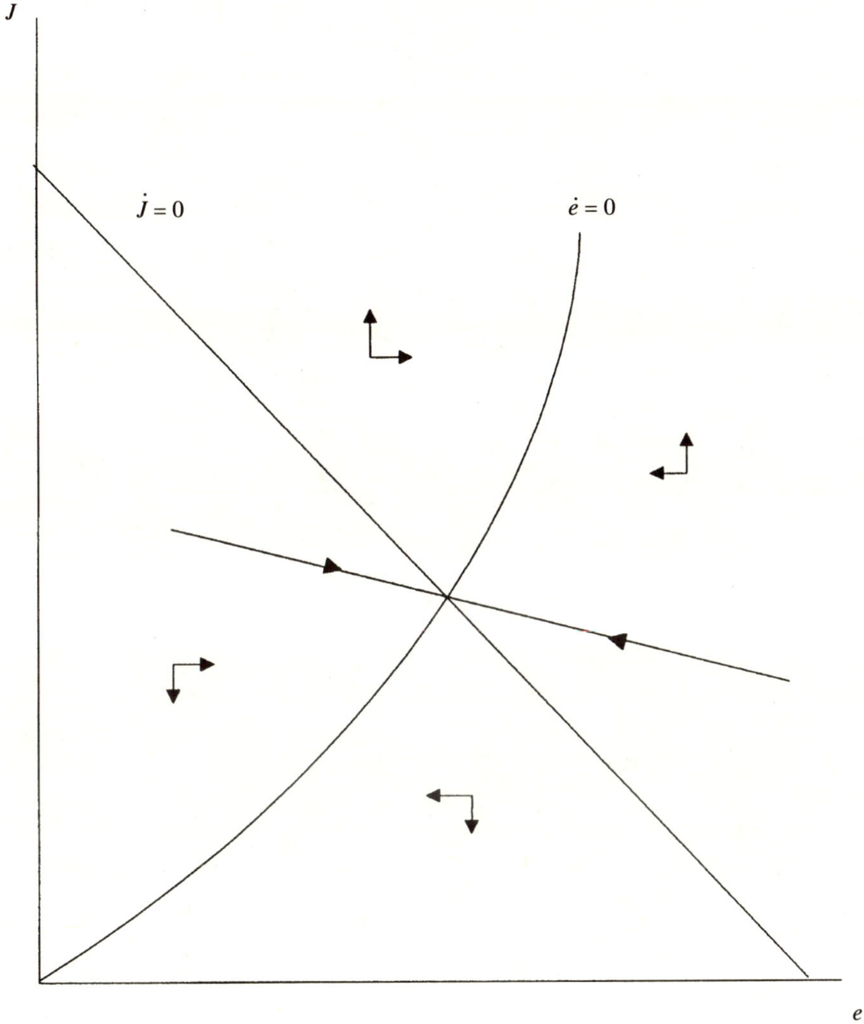

Figure 2.1
Saddle-path stability in a search model

constant returns to scale. The condition for the constant J locus to slope upwards – as required for multiple intersections with the stationary locus for employment – amounts to the requirement that an increase in the average rate at which individuals exit unemployment raises the wage and lowers profits. This holds for both the efficiency-wage and the insider-outsider models, but not for the

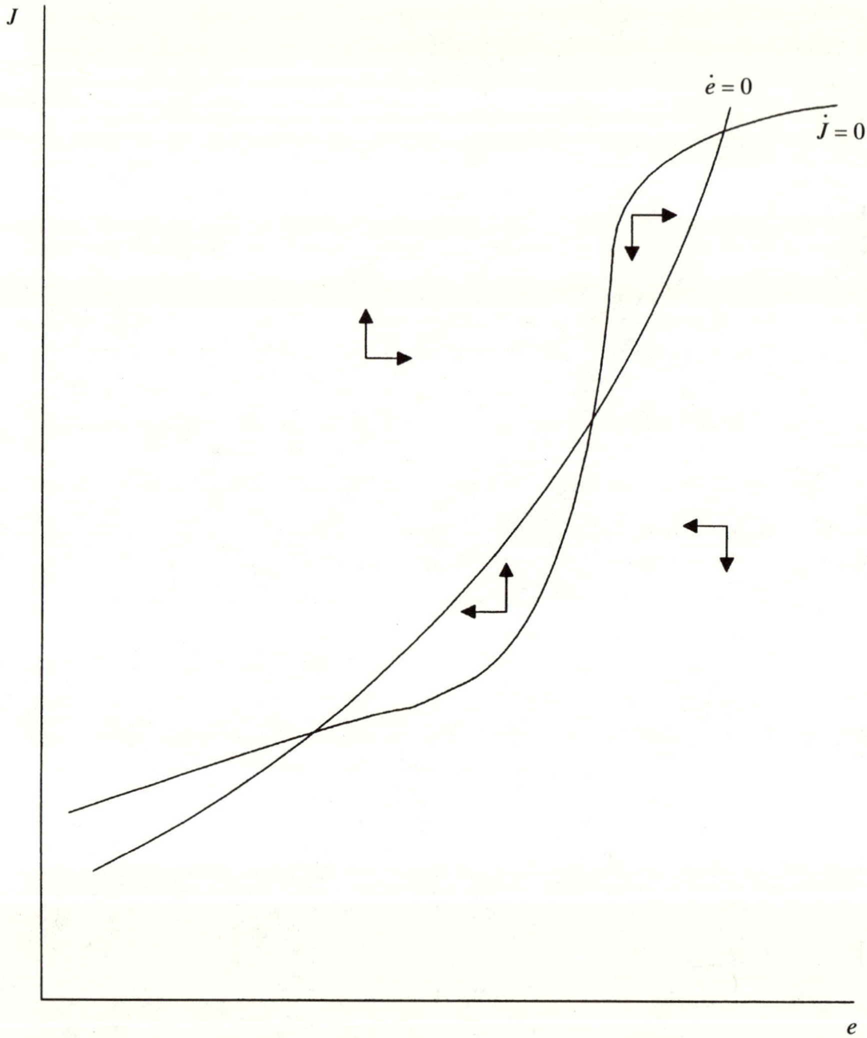

Figure 2.2
Multiple equilibria in a search model

competitive. Given this, the results are qualitatively the same as for the model driven by increasing returns of the production technology, though the mechanism involved is rather different. Here, the external economies of matching and exchange mean that profits are positively affected by the level of employment. If firms expect good times, the current value of a new hire is high, and, indeed, employment will rise. Conversely, a pessimistic employer attributes little value to an additional employee, recruiting falls off, and, as expected, employment and profits decline.

Overlapping-Generations Models and Multiple Equilibria

Another area of active macroeconomic research that can generate a multiplicity of equilibria is based on variants of Samuelson's overlapping generations (see, for example, the advanced textbook treatment in Blanchard and Fischer 1989, chaps. 3–5). Though such models are not closely tied to the properties of labour markets and the study of hysteresis therein, they are the outcome of a fully optimizing framework that has the potential for dynamic inefficiency. While our discussion is necessarily brief, it does reveal that there is nothing especially arbitrary or ad hoc about models with multiplicity. If anything, the expectation is rather the reverse: only somewhat special conditions lead to a unique equilibrium.

An example of multiplicity and related outcomes in an overlapping-generations model with money is given in Blanchard and Fischer (1989, 245–56). In such a model, with two-period lives and overlapping generations of agents, the dynamic properties of the system can be usefully summarized by the shape of the offer curve that relates agents' first- and second-period optimal levels of consumption as the rate of return between the two periods varies; or, equivalently, by an offer curve that relates excess demand for goods when agents are young to excess supply of goods when they are old. Under conditions that cannot be ruled out by the usual assumptions about preferences and technology, this offer curve can cross the 45-degree line – the characterization of an equilibrium – with either positive or negative slope. In the positive case, the monetary equilibrium is unstable. For negative slope, however, there is first a stable monetary equilibrium. Along many paths, the economy converges to this stable equilibrium, but, given an initial condition, nothing determines which path is followed.[30] Additionally, the conditions for stable equilibrium also amount to conditions that produce deterministic, cyclical solutions; and the existence of cycles of period three (whereby a state is revisited every third period), which are easy to demonstrate in this model, implies the existence of cycles of every order and of chaotic or aperiodic outcomes.[31] Finally, stable monetary equilibria in this economy also admit the possibility of "sunspot equilibria," where the outcome for the economy depends on extraneous uncertainty simply because agents believe that it does.

In conclusion, the range of results from a simple overlapping-generations model of the macroeconomy undercuts any expectation that equilibrium will "usually" be unique or that only complicated and contrived models lead to multiplicity. Rather, this framework, and its natural extensions (e.g. Grandmont 1985; 1989), give a presumption of non-uniqueness in the general case.

Imperfect Competition and Multiple Natural Rates

One related set of ideas is that multiplicity of equilibria can arise as a consequence of less-than-perfect competition. While not all models with imperfect competition (of some sort) give rise to such multiplicity, other conditions, such as increasing returns being required, display a notable family resemblance within many of these models.[32] I focus here on models exposited by Dixon (1988), Frank (1990), and Manning (1990; 1992).

Dixon bases his theory on a model with oligopolistic firms that set prices and unions that set wages. With two industries, the model specializes to duopoly in the product market and monopoly in the labour market for each industry or sector, and Dixon uses Nash's notion of equilibrium. Government policy is taken as exogenous, and each union sets its nominal wage while taking the other's as given; each does, however, allow for the effect that its own wage-setting will have on firms' employment (and price) decisions in the next round of decision-making. The result is a notion of involuntary unemployment and, most important for present purposes, a continuum of equilibria that Dixon terms the "natural range of employment." In fact, his theory has a unique equilibrium: given a particular level and (sectoral) pattern of government spending, the Nash equilibrium between the two monopoly unions is unique. With the natural range, however, different levels of government spending, or different inter-industry patterns of a fixed total level of spending, will produce varying equilibrium levels of aggregate employment. In contrast, with competitive behaviour, such policy changes would not affect the (invariant) natural rate.

Frank's (1990) model has instead a set of distinct multiple equilibria that arise from risk aversion on the part of monopolistic competitors facing a technology with diminishing returns to scale. The amount of required risk premium (that must be added to the marginal cost of production) depends on the state of the economy, with a low level of activity depressing profits and hence mandating a high risk premium. This feedback leads to self-sustaining recessions even without constant or increasing returns to scale in the technology. The multiple equilibria in this case can be ranked in a Paretian sense.

Finally, Manning's two models (1990, 1992) build on the familiar monopolistic-competition framework, using increasing returns as the driving mechanism that produces multiplicity. Relative to previous work, this theory offers two central innovations. First, Manning addresses long-run equilibrium where the capital stock is allowed to vary, thus making increasing returns perhaps more appealing than when, with a fixed capital stock, it is conceived to be increasing returns to labour alone. Second, especially in the latter paper, Manning is able to implement the approach empirically. I return to discussion of this in chapter 3.

Macroeconomic Models with Non-ergodic Growth

Our final variant of multiple-equilibrium modelling stems from recent work on endogenous growth in an explicitly stochastic environment. In a series of papers, Durlauf (1991a; 1991b; 1993) has presented a variety of abstract models of this type, with technological complementarities among sectors creating the potential for "coordination failures" that compound through time with consequences for long-run growth.[33] The results show patterns of volatility of output across sectors and through time and, in a departure relative to much work on multiplicity, permit some analysis of dynamic processes leading from one equilibrium to another. Of course, such theories remain at some distance from empirical implementation, but, as with many of the other models employing multiple equilibria, they reinforce the idea that uniqueness of equilibrium might better be viewed as the exception, rather than the norm.

CONCLUSION

This chapter has summarized a large number of theories of why past unemployment can affect the natural rate of unemployment, some based explicitly on the behaviour of individuals or groups, and some based more anonymously on interactions in markets characterized by the potential for multiple equilibria. My suspicion is that the stark theoretical results of simple insider-outsider models will not be sustained in deeper analysis and hence that these models will not enjoy continued popularity as a framework for the analysis of hysteresis. Whether other theories based on the duration of unemployment and its effects have lasting influence is a more open question, I feel, and it may be one to which the course of actual events will influence the answer. I believe, in contrast, that we have only begun to scratch the surface of understanding models with multiple equilibria and that their empirical analysis remains quite exploratory. Whether based explicitly on matching and general equilibrium search analysis or on other mechanisms behind macro-economic coordination, the results that may be available from such theories of multiplicity seem a rich vein to mine.[34]

In terms of research achievements to date, it did not seem easy to formulate a microeconomic model that gave rise to a clear prediction of hysteresis while being consistent with a reasonable interpretation of optimization and that was empirically plausible on a priori grounds. However, we can proceed by moving beyond such general notions of intuitive plausibility and examine the empirical evidence that has been marshalled to date. Chapters 3 and 4 address this literature in light of this opening theoretical survey.

3 International Evidence

This chapter surveys the main components of the existing empirical literature on the assessment of hysteresis in labour markets. For purposes of exposition, and also partly because Canada has some distinctive institutional features not present elsewhere, this chapter covers evidence for countries other than Canada. Chapter 4 examines Canadian evidence in detail.

I begin by assessing work on the univariate properties of time series, such as a measure of national income or the unemployment rate. I argue that this literature is largely inconclusive and that, as a matter of common sense, it is not reasonable to think that the rate of unemployment literally obeys a unit-root process. I then study research that looks at a number of series jointly, rather than the univariate approach of the unit-root work, and that assesses whether traditional Phillips curves should allow for hysteresis in the natural rate. Such allowance typically leads to changes in the rate of unemployment markedly affecting the rate of inflation, rather than the traditional level effect, and testing has proceeded along these lines.

I turn next to evaluation of a number of microeconomic-based studies, beginning with the seminal work of Blanchard and Summers (1986), that examine wage and employment determination as motivated by the insider-outsider modelling discussed in the preceding chapter. I then look at a small literature that has developed on testing for multiplicity of equilibria, noting that the restrictions required to generate testable, observable implications from this work are generally quite strong. Finally, I discuss work on the distinctive role of the long-term unemployed and, more broadly, of the importance of duration-dependence in unemployment as a possible microeconomic foundation for macroeconomic hysteresis.

UNIVARIATE PROPERTIES OF TIME SERIES

Beginning with Nelson and Plosser (1982), the past decade has seen reinterpretation of the time series properties of many macroeconomic magnitudes. While it used to be conventional wisdom that real gross national product (GNP) was well described by some sort of low-order autoregressive process around a deterministic trend,[1] a substantial though controversial literature has argued that a better characterization is that real GNP has a unit root. With GNP interpreted thus, temporary output shocks can have a permanent effect, and the traditional decomposition into trend and fluctuations about that trend may be seriously misleading. Notable contributions in this debate include Campbell and Mankiw (1987), Cochrane (1988), De Long and Summers (1988), Shapiro and Watson (1988), Blanchard and Quah (1989), Durlauf (1989), and Christiano and Eichenbaum (1990), and a useful overview is given by Hamilton (1994, especially 444–7).

From the perspective of work on hysteresis, this debate poses three critical issues. First, there remains considerable disagreement over the appropriate characterization of the time-series properties of real GNP, with some tests accepting a unit root and others rejecting it. Campbell and Perron (1991) survey the issues involved in many of these procedures, a key conclusion from this work being that prior knowledge of and appropriate allowance for deterministic trends are necessary prerequisites for testing.[2] Second, some researchers have sought to quantify the importance of the permanent component in GNP, seeing the problem not as a choice between the two polar extremes of stationarity and non-stationarity but rather as a question of the size of the unit root component. However, Quah (1992) has questioned the way in which many have attempted to measure this permanent component, arguing that unless a researcher can explicitly identify the disturbances that drive GNP, such quantification of transitory and permanent components founders on a problem of identification. Existing work has (implicitly) assumed a single disturbance or a structure of disturbances with a particular and restrictive restriction on its serial correlation; neither assumption seems satisfactory.[3]

Third, implications of studies of the time-series properties of real GNP do not necessarily carry over to the rate of unemployment. The theoretical basis of an absence of mean-reverting behaviour for national income is typically given by a model of technological driving shocks to productivity, and there is no reason to think that such shocks would lead to a non-stationary unemployment rate. After all, secular increases in productivity over the medium to long term have not been associated with any particular trend behaviour for unemployment. Thus hysteresis of the unemployment rate is, in many respects, a stronger property than non-stationarity of national income. Most important, it seems clear that a literal unit-root model of the rate of unemployment makes no sense. There is no possibility that the rate will drop to zero or rise to 100 per cent, no matter how far out into the future the series is followed, in contradiction to the predictions of a linear unit-root model. That is, to the extent that univariate work finds evidence that resembles unit-root behaviour, it is perhaps best thought of as a local linear approximation to a globally non-linear system, in which the long-run boundary behaviour of unemployment is not implausible.

With this qualification, I briefly mention two studies that do look internationally at persistence in labour-market series. Barro (1988) examines the univariate properties of annual unemployment rates for 19 countries since 1945,[4] estimating an autoregressive-moving average (ARMA) model with one autoregressive component and a number (termed "k") of moving average terms as required to whiten the residuals from the process; typically, an ARMA (1,1) was estimated. Barro's interpretation is that the autoregressive term is an indicator of the degree of unemployment persistence. Of the 19 countries, 15 have a point estimate for this AR1 coefficient in excess of 0.8, with most lying insignificantly below unity at a 5 per cent level, according to a standard Dickey-Fuller test. However, Barro points out that the joint hypothesis that all the coefficients are equal to unity can be rejected by these data. Furthermore, the evidence from early periods is markedly less indicative of persistence. The

Canadian results are an AR1 coefficient (standard error) of 0.881 (0.073) for the period 1948–86; for 1920–38, the figures are 0.724 (0.124).

Phaneuf (1988, Tableau 2) examines an empirical model of the rate of unemployment that allows for an intercept, one autoregressive and moving average parameter, and a deterministic trend component. Using data for 1957–87 for Canada, the United States, Japan, and four European economies, he finds, except for the United States, evidence in favour of a unit root in the unemployment rate. However, the results for Canada, Japan, and the United Kingdom are quite sensitive to the presence of a trend in the estimating equation. Again, the question remains of how such findings should be interpreted in the light of our expectations about the long-run properties of the unemployment rate.

MACROECONOMETRIC STUDIES OF PERSISTENCE AND PHILLIPS CURVES

Another area of macroeconomic study of hysteresis has arisen partly in response to the early observations that provoked development of the idea of labour-market hysteresis. In the face of substantial unemployment, inflation in many European economies showed no sign of abating, suggesting that a natural rate of unemployment, interpreted as a NAIRU, had risen concomitantly with the increase in the actual rate of unemployment. In many macroeconomic models, this link from labour markets to the rate of wage and price inflation is at the foundation of the treatment of aggregate supply, and, adjusted for suitable treatment of inflationary expectations, it remains the basis for the study of Phillips curves.

Gordon (1988; 1989) has developed clear implications for estimation of an empirical Phillips curve in the presence of hysteresis. Suppose that the natural rate of unemployment at a particular date depends both on structural or demographic factors and on the past value of the actual rate of unemployment. Then a Phillips curve relating the rate of inflation, given inflationary expectations, to a measure of the gap between the actual and the natural rates of unemployment implies that both the level and the change in the rate of unemployment should enter into the specification to be estimated. Under "full hysteresis," whereby the past rate of unemployment affects the natural rate with a coefficient of unity and there is hence no unique natural rate, Gordon's work implies that the *level* of the unemployment rate should be an insignificant determinant of the rate of inflation while the *change* in the rate should be significant. Thus full hysteresis would imply that a decrease in the actual rate of unemployment would lead to an increase in inflation, as would be implied by a standard natural-rate model. However, with full hysteresis, this increase in inflation would be finite, as the natural rate itself fell in response to the decline in the actual rate. Full hysteresis, then, is in many respects an "optimistic" view, at least when compared with the difficult supply-side adjustments that seem mandated by the traditional NAIRU interpretation of simultaneously high unemployment and inflation.

Overall, the empirical results of Gordon's procedure are rather mixed. Both his 1988 and his 1989 papers deal with (the detrended logarithm of) output and an output gap rather than with unemployment and its deviation from a natural rate, principally because pre-1939 data are scarce and unreliable. In the former study, "Europe" in the period 1963–86 displays an output ratio that is an insignificant determinant of the change in the gross domestic product (GDP) deflator, whether or not the coefficient on this change variable is allowed to vary before and after 1973. The change in this output ratio over the full period, however, is significantly different from zero at the 1 per cent level, provided this change is entered into the equation with a one-year lag. However, results from a variety of equations are not reported, so it is difficult to evaluate whether or not the conclusion is robust in its response to minor changes in timing and other details of specification.

In the 1989 study, which covers the United States, the United Kingdom, France, West Germany, and Japan for varying though uniformly long periods,[5] Gordon allows for asymmetric effects around a natural rate, so that the coefficient on the level of output can differ between (exogenously specified) periods of high and low output. He further allows for some time variation in the coefficients and includes controls for various types of government intervention in price determination. The main conclusion is that an effect from the level of output is certainly present for Japan and France; for both countries, symmetry cannot be rejected. For the other three countries, Gordon finds asymmetric effects on the level of output; for the United States and the United Kingdom, the effect is clearly larger for positive than for negative values, while the opposite seems true for West Germany. Overall, these long time-series results reject full hysteresis for each of the five countries, though the finding that deep recessions have had only small effects on prices in both the United States and the United Kingdom remains important.

Some related evidence is provided by Cross, Hutchinson, and Yeoward (1990a), who examine American and British data over long periods (1890–1986 and 1855–1986, respectively). In an encompassing framework, they contrast several special cases of a general unrestricted form relating prices to two own lags (i.e. lagged values of prices themselves) and to two lags of unemployment. These cases are a general Phillips curve that restricts the coefficients on lagged price levels, a natural-rate hypothesis that further restricts the labour market's influence to a contemporaneous effect on levels, and a hysteresis hypothesis that instead restricts such influence to a change effect, analogous to Gordon's treatment. The main results are that the hysteresis variant appears to outperform the other restrictions according to a number of tests. However, the authors note that such a specification none the less shows important problems with serial correlation and heteroskedasticity. Indeed, the estimates of the unrestricted model correspond to an equilibrium-difference equation for prices with the largest root greater than unity, which would imply an unstable price level. This finding suggests that undue weight not be placed on these apparently fragile results.

Another multi-country study of macroeconomic unemployment persistence is Alogoskoufis and Manning (1988a),[6] which begins by estimating a second-order, autoregressive model of the unemployment rate for each of 14 countries for most of the period since the Second World War.[7] The sum of these coefficients varies from two cases of 1.04 to one of 0.48, with the broad pattern being that this sum is close to one in non-Nordic European economies and is much less, typically close to one-half, in the Nordic economies and in the United States. The authors break down this reduced-form model of unemployment persistence into a number of logically distinct components: membership dynamics and wage-setting behaviour, persistence of real-wage aspirations, and persistence of labour demand driven by factors such as adjustment costs and institutional restrictions on layoff practices. In some cases, knowledge of the two autoregressive parameters for the unemployment-rate process can be used to determine which structural process is at work, though clearly not all such structural coefficients are identified. Using auxiliary evidence on labour-demand elasticities from other studies, the authors conclude that the United States has very low wage persistence and, apparently, very low costs of adjustment of labour demand; both results stand in sharp contrast to their European evidence.

In no country does there seem to be a major role for insider-outsider dynamics of wage-setting; the evidence for such effects is, if anything, slightly stronger in the United States, where, of course, the overall degree of unemployment persistence is that much lower. However, the authors, in their attention to the causes of persistence, relative to a natural rate, eschew any modelling of the demographic and other determinants of that natural rate. They thus attribute all changes in unemployment to the persistence-generating mechanisms that they highlight, when in fact some (though perhaps not all) of the changes in the period 1952–85 might better be thought of as responses of the equilibrium unemployment rate to evolving, underlying structural determinants.[8]

Finally, Ball (1993) has developed a procedure for measuring a "sacrifice ratio" – the ratio of the undiscounted output loss to the fall in the inflation rate – that allows estimates to be obtained for each disinflationary event, rather than averaging macroeconomic performance across a long time series and rather than averaging the output-inflation tradeoff over periods of both disinflation and expansion. Defining a disinflationary episode as a period starting at an inflation peak and ending in a trough with the inflation rate at least two percentage points below the preceding peak, Ball identifies 28 such episodes in nine countries using annual data for 1960–91.[9] Trend movement of output is removed from the series by his assumptions that output equals trend both at the inflation peak (when there is no change in the rate of inflation) and four quarters after the inflation trough and that trend output grows log-linearly between these points. Annual data thus yield average sacrifice ratios between 0.32 (Australia) and 2.52 (United States) (with a value of –0.23 for Japan), while quarterly data range from 0.75 (France) to 2.92 (West Germany). The Canadian results give 0.99 for the 1969–70 disinflation, 0.38 for 1974–76, and 2.23 for 1981–85.[10] Ball then uses these figures to assess the determinants of the sacrifice ratio, suggesting that the speed of disinflation is important:

gradualism makes disinflation *more* costly.[11] Also, the costs of disinflation are lower in countries with more flexible labour contracts, suggesting an important role for wage-determination behaviour. (Below I examine a number of studies that investigate this link further.) Note, though, that Ball's procedure of removing trend components does implicitly assume that trend output is left unaffected by disinflation, which would not be valid in the presence of hysteresis. Although Ball is aware of this issue (p. 7) and suggests that his results on the relative costs of different disinflations would likely be robust in response to a change in the trend, the presence of hysteresis would radically alter the absolute size of his figures.

MICROECONOMIC-BASED STUDIES OF WAGE DETERMINATION

In addition to the macroeconomic analyses discussed above, there have been a number of attempts to study the microeconomics of wage and employment determination, focused around the membership dynamics inherent in the insider-outsider model first stressed by Blanchard and Summers (1986). In practice, some of this testing has used aggregated data, so the distinction with respect to the studies covered above is that the present work is often grounded more in some sort of microeconomic basis. I first discuss the evidence from Blanchard and Summers's original paper, then briefly examine various extensions.[12]

The basic structure for testing, which turns out to be quite close to that adopted on macroeconomic grounds by Gordon, can be exposited in a few equations. Labour demand is assumed to be given by

$$n = sn_{-1} - (1 - s)b(w - p) + e, \qquad (3.1)$$

where n is employment, $w - p$ the real wage, and e a random-walk term. This formulation of adjustment cost neglects, for the sake of simplicity, the role of expected future real wages on labour demand. The union determines expected employment as

$$En = (1 - a)\, n^* + an_{-1}, \qquad (3.2)$$

where $a = 1$ implies hysteresis and $a = 0$ means history-*in*dependence. Lastly, the simplest stochastic specification is that the wage is given by the target wage w^* that solves (3.2) together with a disturbance term so that

$$w = w^* + u, \tag{3.3}$$

where the error term u has zero mean and is serially uncorrelated. When these components are put together, this basic model yields a wage and an employment equation. Using the latter with the labour demand equation, one can generate a reduced-form wage equation as follows:

$$\begin{aligned} w - w_{-1} &= \mathrm{k} + (Ep - p_{-1}) \\ &+ ((1 - s)/b)^{-1} [(1 + s - a)n_{-1} - sn_{-2}] + v, \end{aligned} \tag{3.4}$$

where v is a composite-error term[13] and k is a constant depending on b, s, a, and n^*. An ordinary, least-squares estimate of this equation will be consistent, given the assumptions above, and the (absolute value of the) ratio of the coefficient on lagged employment to that on the second lag of employment should equal unity under hysteresis.

Blanchard and Summers's (1986) results using this approach seem quite robust across a number of specifications, including alternative timing assumptions and lag structures, inclusion or exclusion of a time trend, use of unemployment in place of employment in the reduced-form wage equation, and inclusion or exclusion of lagged real wages, the capital-labour ratio, an indicator of oil price changes, and a measure of productivity growth. Over the period 1953–84, the evidence for France, the United Kingdom, and West Germany is of substantial persistence, with the ratio of the two employment (or unemployment) coefficients often being high and close to unity. In contrast, the US evidence shows much less hysteresis, with the ratio of the coefficients being around one-half. As the authors note, however, the first-order autoregressive process for employment or unemployment implied by the theoretical model and used in the estimation does not adequately capture the time-series properties of the data,[14] possibly because of a difference in the periodicity of the theory relative to the annual data used in estimation.[15]

Subsequent work has clarified the extent to which these estimates can be given a hysteretic structural interpretation. Kennan (1988) in particular considers a number of equilibrium interpretations of wage and employment fluctuations, and the model of hysteresis in Blanchard and Summers (1986) is a special case of Kennan's general framework. If we make some assumptions on the nature of shocks to labour demand and the union's target-employment equation, the model amounts to a second-order vector autoregression (VAR) with two restrictions: that the wage equation excludes its own twice-lagged value and that the wage does not Granger-cause employment.[16] Making these assumptions, and using data for a number of countries, Kennan demonstrates that this restricted VAR can identify the structural parameters of this hysteresis model. The figures for the hysteresis parameter are quite close to one, ranging from 0.888 (Denmark, 1972–86) to 0.994 (Japan, 1953–85); the Canadian figure for 1954–86 is 0.989. However, in interpreting these results, some other, problematic aspects of Kennan's results should be noted. First, much naturally depends on the process for the two disturbances, which are assumed to be AR1. Second, the estimates of all the demand parameters are very imprecise and are often incorrectly signed; the estimated adjustment cost is negative in the US case, for example.

A number of other papers have pursued these ideas, studying the role of insiders in wage determination.[17] Coe (1990) gives evidence from 14 countries using industry-level data and finds that the annual evolution of employment at this level does indeed resemble a random walk; this work extends that of Nickell and Wadhwani (1990). However, his results reveal little difference in industry-level hysteresis effects in wage-setting between North America and Europe, though the latter has far greater unemployment. Nickell and Kong (1992) also use industry-level data for Britain and find that, though insider effects have some influence, significant evidence of hysteresis is present only in a small minority of industries.

TESTING FOR MULTIPLICITY OF EQUILIBRIA

In contrast to the areas discussed above, there has been comparatively little testing for multiplicity of equilibria. As noted in the survey of theoretical approaches in chapter 2, this research places little explicit restriction on the dynamic process by which an economy moves to one equilibrium rather than another. Consequently, the problem facing the empirical researcher is how to determine, in the absence of knowledge of such a selection mechanism, whether the economy has "jumped" from one equilibrium to another, or whether a particular equilibrium has altered in response to changed fundamentals. In general terms, the econometric problems raised by this issue are severe, since the presumption in all Cowles-type structural specifications is that, given the exogenous data,[18] the endogenous variables can be determined uniquely. It is precisely this presumption that is invalid in the presence of multiple equilibria. Jovanovic (1989) gives a general, abstract treatment of these econometric issues for models that display multiple equilibria, showing that it is very difficult to obtain observable implications without making quite strong assumptions about the selection mechanism whereby the economy chooses one equilibrium rather than another.

One example of the procedures following from these results is Dagsvik and Jovanovic (1991), who use a very restrictive model where a money surprise is the only exogenous variable and where the only endogenous variable is employment. They parameterize a simple model economy so that one regime has a unique equilibrium for all values of the exogenous variable, while the other has some realizations of the exogenous variables that yield the potential for three distinct equilibria. The selection mechanism they examine is Markovian[19] if, in the preceding period, the economy was in the regime with multiplicity; otherwise, when moving from the unique equilibrium regime to one with three equilibria, the probability that a particular outcome is chosen is taken to be the steady-state probability from the Markov chain for that branch.

The results from maximum-likelihood estimation of this simple model are in many ways surprising. Using US data divided into three partly overlapping periods – 1901–40, 1921–40, and 1951–86 – they find that, in each period, uniqueness performs better than the model with multiplicity, in terms of the value of the likelihood. Indeed, even where they examine the local maximum under the restriction that the economy is governed by the regime with multiplicity, for each period the same branch of the equilibrium correspondence is chosen (and, oddly, this branch is unstable). The apparent conclusion is that uniqueness robustly outperforms multiplicity, but with at least two qualifications. First, the parameter whose sign determines into which regime the economy falls is never significantly different from zero in the maximum-likelihood estimates. Second, the results could be invalid if the a priori specification of the equilibrium-selection mechanism is incorrect. The authors note that a mechanism that allowed a role for past values of the exogenous variable would be less easily rejected (and could be sensible if, for example, the recent actions of the central bank operate to signal an equilibrium to be chosen in the current period). However, whether (and how) one can implement this idea without losing identification of the model remains an open question.

Three papers that use alternative methods to address the potential for multiplicity are Pissarides (1986), Carruth and Oswald (1988), and Manning (1991). Pissarides (1986) studies the joint properties of unemployment and vacancies to estimate a matching function and to test for increasing returns to scale, this being one condition for multiplicity in the theoretical literature on matching surveyed in the preceding chapter. He finds no evidence of important increasing returns using British data.[20] Recent work on the United States by Blanchard and Diamond (1989) corroborates this finding, at least in the ordinary, least-squares estimates that they discuss.[21] Carruth and Oswald (1988) find analogous results with two quite different procedures. First, they specify a fairly conventional, two-equation model, the novelty being that in both the labour demand and the real-wage specifications the model includes logarithmic polynomials in the key endogenous variables. This empirical strategy, with each equation being estimated separately, allows for non-monotonicity and hence for the possibility of multiple intersections, corresponding to multiple equilibria. Second, they estimate a two-sector model of Nash equilibrium in wages,[22] which also admits the possibility of multiplicity. In both cases, and again perhaps surprising, British data for 1964–83 fail to support multiplicity. The labour demand curve does seem to be S-shaped, according to their estimates, but the estimated-wage equation is always increasing in employment and always intersects the labour-demand curve in the downward-sloping region, where equilibrium must be unique. In the Nash model of interdependent wages, there is similarly some sign of non-linearity mattering, in that the reaction functions have an inverted U-shape. Again, however, the estimated intersection is in a region where both curves slope upward, where uniqueness is assured, and where, at least on the basis of a naïve adjustment process, this unique equilibrium is stable.

In contrast, Manning (1991) specifies an explicit structural model of imperfect competition in the labour market that allows for multiple equilibria caused by increasing returns to scale. He estimates this structural model using annual British data for 1951–87 and concludes that, with the capital stock taken as given, the parameter values imply a unique equilibrium. However, when the capital stock is allowed to vary in the long run, this conclusion is reversed, and the economy appears best characterized by multiplicity. This conclusion must be tempered on two counts, however. First, as is often the case with structural estimation, one cannot be sure that the identifying assumptions are valid. Second, because of the similar performances of the single- and multiple-equilibrium versions of the model, Manning cannot decisively reject a unique natural rate.

A related paper by Stock (1991) considers the possibility that the degree of autocorrelation of the rate of unemployment may depend on the level of unemployment, so that greater persistence is found in recessions. This idea leads not to the "non-linear" business-cycle literature (e.g., Neftçi 1984) but rather to the specification of a non-linear, first-order autoregressive model, which is estimated using the "time-deformation" methods developed in Stock (1987; 1988). The results suggest the presence of important non-linearities, though for both the United States and the United Kingdom the main finding is unexpectedly one of lower serial correlation of unemployment in recessions than in booms. Vis-à-vis multiplicity, Stock interprets his results as showing reduced dependence in the unemployment rate when unemployment has been rising and increased dependence when it has been stable, which may suggest shifts between multiple equilibria that each display persistence. However, moving from this possibility to a model with multiple equilibria and testable, observable implications remains difficult, as the other papers reveal. At best, the conclusion seems to be that the evidence in favour of multiplicity is mixed.

LONG-TERM UNEMPLOYMENT AND DURATION DEPENDENCE

One particular area of microeconometric investigation that is relevant to the underlying determinants of hysteresis is the literature on state dependence in unemployment. Clearly presented by Heckman and Borjas (1980), state dependence arises in three forms – the probability that a spell continues beyond a certain date may variously change with its elapsed length (duration dependence); depend on the incidence (but not necessarily the length) of past spells of the same type (occurrence dependence); or depend on the length(s) of past spell(s) of this type (lagged duration dependence). Most interest has centred on duration dependence, though some empirical work has addressed the other variants.

One central problem that will be sketched here is to distinguish true state dependence from spurious dependence produced by failure to control adequately for heterogeneity in the population. To illustrate in a simple example, suppose that each individual in a given population has a constant probability per period of leaving unemployment, no matter how long the unemployment spell may have lasted. That is, we suppose that there is no true duration dependence.[23] However, assume further that these probabilities, which are constant through time for each individual, vary across individuals, but that this heterogeneity is unobservable (or, at least, cannot be fully controlled for by conditioning on observables such as sex, age, education, and region). What will happen through time as a number of these individuals start unemployment spells? Clearly, at any point into the spell, those with the higher per-period probabilities of leaving unemployment are more likely to do so, while those with the lower probabilities are less likely to do so. As a result, there is sorting of the individuals, with those left unemployed for longer and longer being, on average, those with the lowest chances of getting work. Thus the observable consequence of this unobserved heterogeneity will be duration dependence, with the average exit rate falling as realized unemployment spells lengthen. The separation of such spurious dependence from its true counterpart is a key issue; further notable analysis is contained in Heckman and Singer (1984), Han and Hausman (1990), Heckman (1991), and Sueyoshi (1992), while Kiefer's (1988) survey covers a broad range of the contributions in this area.

To give examples of substantive results on state dependence, Moffitt (1985) and Meyer (1990) both use data obtained from state unemployment insurance (UI) administrators that illustrate the nature of this research, though chapter 4, below, looks further at the Canadian situation. Moffitt's analysis of the empirical hazard finds time-to-exhaustion effects from UI to be U-shaped, while Meyer's non-parametric estimation of the baseline hazard leads to an estimated four- or five-fold increase in the hazard associated with an expected lapsing of benefits. In terms of the empirical Kaplan-Meier hazard, however, Meyer's Figure 3 (1990, 763) shows a relatively flat hazard out to over 20 weeks of unemployment, followed by a noisy but generally rising hazard thereafter.[24]

Finally, I mention two other areas of work. First, one set of literature addresses, with varying degrees of success, the question of longer-term effects from early unemployment experiences. Rather than focusing on specific duration dependence within a spell, some of this work suggests that patterns of unemployment and insecure employment early in working life can have effects long into a career. Ellwood (1982), the clearest exploration of this view, contrasts "permanent scars" and "temporary blemishes," concluding that, while poor employment in teenage years is associated with a chequered pattern later in life, much of this effect was accounted for by heterogeneity in the population under study, leaving only a small net effect caused by experience dependence (1982, 383). Though not without weaknesses, especially with regard to the ability of the data to differentiate the competing hypotheses correctly (see Willis's 1982 comment), this broad conclusion has stood up in light of more recent work.

Second, there remain the brute facts of the extent of long-term unemployment in many European economies and of its rise in the past decade or so (see, for example, Rahman and Gera 1991, Table 8.4, p. 103).[25] British long-term unemployment rose from 21.8 per cent of total unemployment in 1979–80 to 41.9 per cent by 1986–88.[26] For West Germany, the figures are 18.5 per cent to 32.0 per cent over the same years. While the Canadian figures are markedly lower, as I discuss in chapter 4, being of the order of 10 per cent by the mid-1980s, the change in many European economies remains striking, and many[27] concur with the general thrust of Layard and Nickell (1986; 1991), Jackman and Layard (1987; 1991), Hughes and Hutchinson (1988), Cross, Hutchinson, and Yeoward (1990b), Winter (1991), and others, who claim that this change must help explain the secular rise in unemployment.[28]

CONCLUSION

The general conclusion that follows from the range of evidence from many countries surveyed in this chapter is that the evidence on the hysteresis hypothesis is at best mixed. While not wishing to place undue emphasis on the univariate analysis – which, as argued, may not be very informative – I would emphasize that the multivariate macroeconomic studies also failed to find clear evidence in favour of hysteresis in many cases. The long time series used in Gordon's work, for example, will probably help in assessment of a claim about the long-run properties of the interrelationship between two series, and failure to discover evidence of hysteresis there is significant. Similarly, the microeconomic analyses of wage determination generated no unambiguous set of results, with some questions remaining about the structural interpretation of the apparently hysteretic results. Also, while much of the microeconometric literature on state dependence in its various forms addresses separation of heterogeneity and true dependence – "sorting" versus "scarring," in Osberg's (1993) terms – it does not seem that strong evidence is available for the types of duration effects that might generate hysteresis. However, various limitations in the data and allowance for non-stationarities introduced by unemployment insurance leave this conclusion qualified. Finally, there remains little doubt that long-term unemployment can at least partly explain changing labour markets in many European economies, though it is less clear that such a phenomenon can lead to hysteresis.

4 Canadian Evidence

The Canadian rate of unemployment increased dramatically in the 1980s, both relative to its own performance since the Second World War and relative to the US rate of unemployment. National decadal averages moved continuously upward from 4 per cent in the 1950s and 5 per cent in the 1960s to 6.7 per cent in the 1970s and 9.5 per cent in the 1980s. Relative to the US economy, where labour-market performance has also somewhat worsened over time, the Canadian economy experienced an unemployment rate that averaged two percentage points higher than the US rate during the 1980s, with the gap reaching almost four percentage points in 1984. Prompted in large measure by this divergence in the 1980s – which should be set against the record of the preceding three decades, when Canadian and US unemployment rates were on average very similar – many analysts have sought to explain Canada's deteriorating relative performance. These include Ashenfelter and Card (1986), McCallum (1987), Moorthy (1990), Fortin (1991), Gera (1991), Keil and Symons (1991), Milbourne, Purvis, and Scoones (1991), and Card and Riddell (1993).[1] Some of these researchers have investigated, with mixed results, the idea of hysteresis as applied to Canadian unemployment, while others have offered other explanations of the deterioration in performance.

In this chapter, I first address macroeconomic work, along the lines developed by Gordon and reviewed in the preceding chapter, that looks for a change in the nature of the Phillips curve associated with hysteresis in labour markets. I also mention other macroeconometric work on properties of Canadian time series. I then turn to attempts to model and understand the Canadian natural rate of unemployment, discussing how the interpretation of such efforts must be modified if, indeed, hysteresis is present. I go on to examine a small but influential literature on the distinctive role of the Canadian unemployment insurance system, particularly with regard to the role of regional extended benefits following the high levels of unemployment in the early 1980s. Finally, I consider evidence on the importance of long-term unemployment in Canada, discussing incidence and duration dependence.

MACROECONOMICS OF PHILLIPS CURVES AND TESTING FOR HYSTERESIS

The recent macroeconomic literature on Canadian labour markets analyses the rise in the unemployment rate in the 1980s. With one notable exception, these papers substantially agree; I discuss both the exception and the mainstream view in some detail.

McCallum (1987) is in many ways a precursor to the more recent work, in that he analyses reduced-form unemployment equations that seek to explain the behaviour of an unemployment-gap measure – typically, the divergence between the actual rate of unemployment and some measure of the non-accelerating inflation rate of unemployment (NAIRU) – in terms of a lagged-gap measure and a number of sectoral and aggregate demand variables. Using annual data for Canada (1954–87) and the United States (1957–85 or 1954–85, depending on availability of data), McCallum found an important role for aggregate demand variables in explaining post-1981 movements in aggregate unemployment. For present purposes, however, the most striking finding is the indication of parameter instability in the Canadian case for the latter years under study. Using the estimated equation from 1965–81 to forecast the unemployment gap for the final four years covered, he found that while the increases in unemployment up to 1983 were well predicted, the estimated equation systematically overestimated the decline in unemployment for 1983–85. The conjecture was advanced, though not tested, that this late, unexplained jump in the constant term could reflect, in part, hysteresis. McCallum also discussed the regional aspect of the persistence of unemployment after the 1981–82 recession, conjecturing that oil-based sectoral developments, in so far as they are not fully accounted for by his oil-price variable, could have been influential.

In McCallum (1988), which estimated an empirical Phillips curve using data for 1956–87 with some allowance for non-linear effects of unemployment, the former of the two conjectures was tested and decisively rejected. With various choices of sample period and specification, McCallum found that, in a Phillips curve equation determining the rate of change of hourly wage settlements, the coefficient on the unemployment rate for adult males remained strongly significantly different from zero, even when contemporaneous and lagged first differences of the change in this unemployment rate were also included as explanatory variables. Incidentally, he also found that a convex specification of a Phillips curve permitted satisfactory accounting of the joint behaviour of wages and unemployment after 1981. This result held both for Canada and for the United States, and in both countries rejection of hysteresis was clear-cut.

Fortin (1988; 1989) similarly found little evidence of hysteresis in Canadian unemployment. The earlier paper, which summarized and assessed a number of studies (including McCallum 1988 and Phaneuf 1988) in a special issue of *l'Actualité économique*, concluded that there was evidence that the pace of economic recovery was inherently slow – a theme echoing earlier work such as Tobin's (1972) – and that further investigation with due allowance for changing structural factors was warranted. The later paper, largely an update of the Canadian NAIRU figures in Fortin and Newton (1982), estimated a reduced form-price equation using annual data for 1956–84. When Fortin used the unemployment rate of men aged 25 and over as the indicator of labour-market tightness,[2] he found the results generally satisfactory, with substantial parameter stability over sub-periods and with indication that the null hypothesis of linearity could not be rejected, despite McCallum.

Most important in view of subsequent work, Fortin investigated possible absence of a level effect from the unemployment rate for adult men, including three unrestricted (annual) lags. This version of hysteresis was strongly rejected in favour of a stable NAIRU for men. From the estimated Phillips curve, imposing long-run equilibrium with respect to all price variables and the change in indirect taxes and assuming no wage-price controls in steady state, the male NAIRU is estimated as 4.9 per cent, with an asymptotic standard error of 0.2 per cent.

Confirmation of this finding comes in work at the Bank of Canada by Cozier and Wilkinson (1990; 1991 – the latter a revision of the former). In an attempt to measure the size of the costs of disinflation in Canada, Cozier and Wilkinson formulate an expectations-augmented Phillips curve and impose the so-called accelerationist restriction: that the sum of the coefficients on past inflation equal one.[3] This permits representation of the curve in terms of changes in the rate of inflation, with the present change being determined by a number of past changes, together with a term in the output gap – the deviation of output from some calculation of an equilibrium or potential output level – that turns out to be critical for their calculations.

The key magnitude sought is the "sacrifice ratio" – the output gap necessary to induce a permanent change of one percentage point in the rate of inflation.[4] In this framework, the sacrifice ratio is given by the complement of the sum of the coefficients on the lagged-inflation–change variables, divided by the coefficient on the output gap. Thus, in a specification where both the level and the change of the output gap matter, only the coefficient on the level itself matters for the computation of the sacrifice ratio. The intuition for this is simply that, in looking at the long-run effect, the sacrifice ratio is affected first in one direction and then, in the next period, in the other direction by a coefficient on the change of the gap in output. This clearly matters in evaluating evidence for hysteresis.

The empirical results in Cozier and Wilkinson (1991) largely confirm earlier findings. Based on quarterly data for the period 1963:third quarter (Q3) to 1988:Q4, their estimates in terms of changes in the rate of price inflation (measured by the GDP deflator) allow for changes in commodity prices, crude oil prices, and a dummy variable that indicates (changes in) the operation of the Anti-Inflation Board. When the lagged level and contemporaneous change in the output gap are included in the specification,[5] both variables have positive coefficients that differ significantly from zero.[6] In an alternative formulation, the output level and change variables are replaced by labour-market variables: respectively, a measure of the unemployment gap[7] and the change in the actual unemployment rate. In this case, with all other controls as before, the level coefficient on the unemployment gap is significantly negative, while the change coefficient is negative but differs insignificantly from zero at the 5 per cent level, having an absolute value of its *t*-ratio of 1.71. Since both models have an important level effect, both imply that the sacrifice ratio is well-defined and that the effects of a permanent disinflation are temporary. Calculated from the estimates of the other coefficients in the specification, the output gap formulation gives a sacrifice ratio of 2.1, meaning that the (temporary) lost output from a policy that permanently reduces the rate of inflation by one percentage point is 2.1 per cent. As the authors note, this figure is rather lower than many other estimates in the literature, possibly because of their direct relation of inflation to the output gap[8] and their particular sample period.[9]

Detailed study of one aspect of the robustness of Cozier and Wilkinson's findings was provided recently for nine countries by Lipsett and James (n.d.) in a draft document prepared for the federal Department of Finance. They employ "rolling regressions" of two types to address the stability of estimates of Phillips curves and sacrifice ratios over time: first, by adding another quarterly data point to the sample, which thus enlarges each round; and second, by maintaining a fixed sample size of 13 years of quarterly data, dropping old points as new ones are added. For the full sample period of 1961:Q3 to 1993:Q1, the results yield significant level and change effects on inflation from the output gap when the researchers use a Hodrick-Prescott (H-P) filter to construct trend GDP, though the results using a quadratic in time to construct the trend leads to a significant change effect but a level effect that is significant only at the 10 per cent level.[10] However, using both rolling-regressions approaches (and their preferred H-P filter), the authors find that the level effect of the output gap is always significantly different from zero (except in quarter 1 of 1983), thereby rejecting hysteresis. Canada is unusual in that the sacrifice ratio remains significant throughout the sample period,[11] though the estimate does not stay constant. The Canadian ratio tends to rise over time,[12] though the increases are clearly bunched around economic slack times.

The one remarkable exception to the norm in the Canadian estimates of the Phillips curve and the presence of hysteresis is Fortin (1991), presented as the Innis Lecture at the Annual Meetings of the Canadian Economics Association in June 1991. In this paper, Fortin adopts a specification similar to that used in Fortin (1989), but adds lagged values of the change in the (adult male[13]) unemployment rate. The dependent variable is now the rate of inflation measured as the consumer price index (CPI), excluding food and energy, in accordance with the Bank of Canada's professed target variable,[14] and the annual data cover the period 1957–90.

First, in an assessment of the robustness of the previous work, Fortin restricts attention to 1957–84 and finds little change in the results. The lagged unemployment-change variables are insignificant, the current level has a significantly negative coefficient, and the current change has a significantly positive coefficient. This situation implies negative hysteresis, if anything, and a well-defined natural rate for this demographic group that, at 4.8 per cent, is very close to the analogous figure in Fortin (1989). However, this result appears to change when the sample is extended by adding the six annual observations for 1985–90. In this case, Fortin is able easily to reject parameter stability between the two periods and is led to investigate a potential structural break, which he places in the early 1970s. By allowing some variables in the estimated equation to have different coefficients for the sub-periods 1957–72 and 1973–90, Fortin finds that the results change dramatically.

Imposing price homogeneity, one can reach Fortin's preferred specification (equation 1.4 in his Table 1, 789), which allows the constant term and the coefficients on the contemporaneous unemployment-level and -change terms to differ in the two sub-periods, while introducing the two annual lagged values of the unemployment change term for only 1973–90. This equation displays conventional properties for 1957–72, with mildly negative hysteresis and a natural rate of 4.8 per cent. For 1973–90, however, the level effect of unemployment becomes insignificant, while the current change variable has a coefficient of –0.38 with a standard error of 0.14, giving strong evidence of positive hysteresis. The ratio of the estimated constant term to the estimated coefficient on the level of unemployment – which gives the estimated natural rate from this equation – is 5.9 per cent, which is higher than the earlier figures; but, more important, neither the constant effect nor the level effect is significant for 1973–90. If, taking the next step, one then drops these two variables, the resulting model displays "full" hysteresis, and a short-term change in unemployment has no long-run effect on inflation. That is, Fortin finds a long-run trade-off between inflation and unemployment; changes in inflation are linked to changes in unemployment, and, correspondingly, the same is true for their respective levels.

Fortin is quick both to note that such results are novel and may not be robust and to raise the question of what happened to produce such a sharp break in 1973. He considers four hypotheses – that deep recessions have hysteretical effects (as Gordon found to some degree for the Depression in the United States); that unemployment insurance, which changed radically in Canada following the reforms of 1971, plays a key role; that the post-1972 slowdown in productivity affected hysteresis in some way; and that the divergence in unionization between Canada and the United States may play a role, along the lines originally suggested by Blanchard and Summers.[15] However, none of these candidates seems, in his view, able to account for more than a very small proportion of the change that the preferred specification revealed, leaving the debate somewhat inconclusive.

This line of argument is reiterated in Fortin (1993), a policy-focused paper that summarizes much of the debate on control of inflation and the persistence of unemployment.[16] Using aggregate data for Canada for 1973–90 and for the United States for 1966–90 in an econometric specification that mimics that in his Innis Lecture (Fortin 1991), he finds insignificant unemployment level effects and significant change effects, with the implied point estimate of the degree of hysteresis being 77 per cent for Canada and 81 per cent for the United States (Table 3, p. 12).[17] These results match Fortin's earlier findings for Canada and show that US data yield similar results, given a similar specification.[18] As before, though, Fortin notes major concerns about robustness, given the small time span covered by the data. In addition, he expresses misgivings about the interpretation of such hysteresis results, given apparent failure to find a satisfactory microeconomic or macroeconomic underpinning.[19]

Finally, a number of recent papers from the Bank of Canada have extended the discussion on labour-market hysteresis in Canada. First, a study by Laxton, Shoom, and Tetlow (1992) addresses the potentially important issue of measurement in the assessment of hysteresis. Cozier and Wilkinson (1991, 15) noted that assessment of the sacrifice ratio by estimation of an empirical Phillips curve depended heavily on measurement of the output-gap variable – both its level and its change – which amounted to the question of how to measure the level of potential or equilibrium output. Equivalent issues also arise for characterization of a natural rate of unemployment, of course. To quantify this concern, Cozier and Wilkinson (1991) employed other measures of potential output (in addition to the measure from the Bank of Canada's RDXF model used in their main results) – a linear, a quadratic, and a Hodrick-Prescott trend.[20] The estimates of the sacrifice ratio, based on an equation including both the level and the change of the output gap, were 6.3, 2.6, and 1.2, respectively, compared with 2.1 using the RDXF potential output figure. Neglecting the linear trend, which cannot capture turning points (and for which the point estimate differed insignificantly from zero), these figures were taken as displaying considerable stability.

Laxton, Shoom, and Tetlow (1992) extend this work by conducting a small Monte Carlo simulation, building on earlier work by Laxton and Tetlow. They parameterize a small model economy as consisting of a potential output equation, obeying a random walk with a small drift term; a demand or cyclical component that is summarized by a second-order autoregressive process; and a simple Phillips curve with lagged level and change terms in the output gap. The parameter values for this last equation were taken from Cozier and Wilkinson (1990). The error structure adopted attributes 40 per cent of total output variation to permanent shocks,[21] and the researchers simulate this model economy, using the Hodrick-Prescott filter to measure potential output.

Their results naturally depend on these various assumptions and on the smoothness parameter adopted for the filter generating the potential output measure, but the pattern of findings seems quite robust. The principal conclusion is that the problems in measurement associated with potential output downwardly bias the estimated coefficient on the level of the output gap and upwardly bias the estimated coefficient on the change in the output gap. The intuition is simply that the errors in the level effect – since the potential output filter attributes supply-side shocks to the demand side of the picture – attenuate the level coefficient, while the errors in the measurement of the change in potential output are partially offsetting owing to the first difference. Clearly, this result and intuition are both model-specific, since such problems in measurement do not usually have an unambiguous effect on estimated coefficients. None the less, the findings do at a minimum suggest that, because of problems with both the level and the change variable, econometric estimates of a Phillips curve may be biased towards finding spurious hysteresis.

Two related papers are Laxton, Rose, and Tetlow (1993a; 1993b). In 1993b, the authors conduct a Monte Carlo study of output and inflation with a non-linear Phillips curve, demonstrating that with standard univariate measures of potential output, the econometrician will probably falsely reject non-linearity. Output gaps would be mismeasured in the case of non-linearity,[22] and, unlike the pure measurement error in Laxton, Shoom, and Tetlow (1992), such bias would not cancel on average. In Laxton, Rose, and Tetlow (1993a), these authors employ multivariate filtering to use information about inflation in identifying potential output (and hence the output gap). With a proxy for inflationary expectations from the Conference Board's survey of inflation forecasts, they find evidence of non-linearity in Canadian annual data for 1973–91,[23] echoing earlier results of McCallum (1988) but contrasting with the results (from quarterly data) of Cozier and Wilkinson (1991).[24] One issue that remains open is whether measures of an output gap generated from a non-linear model themselves would yield similar results: those used in Laxton, Rose, and Tetlow (1993a) are produced from a linear specification but are then employed to yield a non-linear preferred model.

Another recent paper that extends the analysis of hysteresis in the Canadian labour market is Poloz and Wilkinson (1992), which addresses a number of robustness questions relating to the studies by Fortin (1991) and Cozier and Wilkinson (1991) and attempts to discover the primary reason(s) for the apparent discrepancy in their results. Since this general approach, though not its detailed implementation, turns out to be quite close to the investigation I perform in chapter 5 below, I defer extended discussion of these new results.

MODELLING OF THE CANADIAN NATURAL RATE

A related literature, which has recently merged with the hysteresis-testing use of empirical Phillips curves reviewed above, examines the determinants of the Canadian natural rate of unemployment.

The contributions relevant for present purposes are Ford and Rose (1989), Burns (1990; 1991a; 1991b), Rose (1990), and Setterfield, Gordon, and Osberg (1992).[25]

Ford and Rose (1989) estimate simultaneously an Okun's-law equation and a Phillips curve, which method avoids having to specify an output gap prior to an unemployment gap, or vice versa. Their results show an important role for demographics in determination of the NAIRU, but comparatively little evidence of a role for parameters of the unemployment insurance (UI) system; overall they give a NAIRU of around 8 per cent by the end of 1987. Rose (1990), in a more extensive survey that also compares Bank of Canada estimates with others in the literature, admits considerable uncertainty about any such numerical estimates. The NAIRU estimate from the Bank's RDXF model, for example, is reported as having a point value of 10.4 per cent,[26] with a 95-per-cent confidence interval being roughly 7.9 per cent to 12.9 per cent. The figures based on system estimation, including an Okun's-law relationship, put the value at between 8.0 and 9.3 per cent by the end of 1987, though Rose notes that such figures are very sensitive to inclusion or exclusion of the years 1982–85, the period of slow recovery following the 1981–82 recession. Similarly, the NAIRU generated by other researchers shows considerable diversity, depending on, among other factors, measurement of inflationary expectations, measurement of changes in wages and/or prices, characterization of the role of the UI system, and the appropriate allowance, if any, for productivity growth.

Burns (1990; 1991a; 1991b) extends this research by looking at the regional dimension in the natural rate, estimating a reduced-form equation for each of the ten provinces by seemingly unrelated regressions. He includes a structural variable related to hysteresis – "HYSTi," defined as the unionization rate of members of the labour force multiplied by the one-period lagged change in the province's unemployment rate. This variable is motivated by the union-based insider-outsider theories of hysteresis and links the role of the change in the unemployment rate discussed above with one alleged prime cause. Empirically, the results do not show much importance for this variable, however, with insignificant results in a majority of provinces and with numerically small results in any event (Burns 1990, Table 7, p. 17).

Finally, the conclusion that point estimates of the natural rate may not be very robust is reinforced by Setterfield, Gordon, and Osberg (1992), who argue that essentially no restrictions are placed on the NAIRU by conventional statistical procedures applied to Canadian macroeconomic data. That is, reasonable specifications of an empirical Phillips curve that satisfy a number of technical criteria (such as absence of serial correlation in the errors and significant coefficients of the appropriate sign) yield a wide range of feasible NAIRU estimates. For the period they examine, 1956–87 in general, such specifications yield figures for the prime-age–male NAIRU ranging from 4.5 per cent to 9.9 per cent. In this period, the actual rate of unemployment for this group ranged from 2.5 per cent to 9.3 per cent. Furthermore, the authors point out that, in addition to this range of point estimates from different specifications, there are standard errors associated with each individual point estimate. In one example, a mid-range estimate of the NAIRU at 6.65 per cent is found to have a large confidence band: within one standard deviation, the figures are 4.18 per cent and 10.33 per cent, which again covers essentially all experience of the actual rate in the same period.

In conclusion, most of these papers do not explicitly discuss how hysteresis can alter the concept of a natural rate. Rather, instead of concentrating on level versus change effects in empirical Phillips curves, they have contrasted point estimates of various conceptions of the natural rate. While full hysteresis would render such a natural rate undefined – it would just follow the actual rate, as in some of the earlier discussion – even without full hysteresis, the confidence intervals around point estimates of the natural rate of unemployment remain very wide.[27]

CANADIAN UNEMPLOYMENT INSURANCE

One distinctively Canadian aspect of recent literature on unemployment persistence and the potential for hysteresis stems from the operation of the Canadian unemployment insurance (UI) system, which of course differs substantially from that in the United States. Though the differential levels of generosity, variously defined, have often been noted in comparisons of the two economies, it has been less clear that any particular change in the degree of generosity can be related to the divergence of Canadian and US unemployment following the recessions of the early 1980s. The principal expansion of Canadian UI came in the 1971 federal act, which does not square well with the timing of the discrepancy in unemployment rates being in the 1980s, though Blank and Card (1991) do suggest that the extent of UI coverage in the United States did drop in the early 1980s.

In an important recent contribution, Milbourne, Purvis, and Scoones (1991) altered the focus of discussion by examining the role of extended UI benefits and a change in UI policy introduced in 1977. This change had two main components. First, it ended "national extended benefits," which in the 1971 legislation had provided for four additional weeks of benefits if the national unemployment rate rose above 4 per cent and for eight additional weeks if it exceeded 5 per cent. Second, it redesigned regional extended benefits, which had provided additional weeks of coverage as a function of the difference between a regional unemployment rate and the national figure, based on local UI benefit regions.[28] The 1977 rules increased eligibility by four weeks for every percentage point that the regional unemployment rate (averaged over the preceding three months) exceeded 4 per cent, up to a maximum of 32 additional weeks (i.e. up to a maximum regional unemployment rate of 12 per cent). With very high unemployment rates in many regions in the early 1980s, this policy dramatically increased the maximum number of weeks of eligibility. Milbourne, Purvis, and Scoones (1991, Figure 4, p. 817), calculate that the national average of maximum number of benefit weeks, weighted by provincial labour-force sizes and allowing for provincial unemployment rates, rises from about 24 weeks in 1981 to about 40 weeks by 1983, with only a slow recovery thereafter.[29] The figure stood in excess of 30 weeks as late as 1987.

Milbourne, Purvis, and Scoones (1991) interpret these calculations in the light of a simple classical microeconomic model of labour supply with voluntary unemployment where, depending on the value of an unobserved taste for consumption/leisure that differs across agents, the population is cleanly divided into three groups. There are non-participants, who never work or receive UI benefits; users of UI benefits who always work for the minimum qualifying period and then collect benefits for the maximum period of eligibility;[30] and employed agents, who always work. It is demonstrated that the critical values for the taste parameter depend on the parameters of the UI system, particularly length of qualifying period and period of eligibility, so that the unemployment rate responds to the type of change in eligibility period produced by the combination of the 1977 legislation and the 1981–82 recession.

If wages are held constant in the model, the longer benefit period raises unemployment duration for (existing) users of the UI system, while also potentially affecting incidence, by reducing incidence among existing users and by raising incidence among previous non-participants. When this model is extended to make the level of wages endogenous, however, the solution for the equilibrium rate of unemployment now depends in an ambiguous way on the period of eligibility. The effect on the wage of lengthening the period can itself be of either sign, and, as a consequence, this expanded subsidy to partial employment can either raise or lower the overall equilibrium unemployment rate.

The empirical work presented by Milbourne, Purvis, and Scoones (1991) is macroeconomic and involves addition of measures of UI parameters to a first-order, autoregressive model of monthly unemployment; longer lag structures were found insignificant.[31] In view of the nature of this empirical implementation, it is probably best to regard the theoretical model as suggestive, though the authors do present one particular (partial adjustment) foundation for their equation. The results show some role for the policy parameters, with the autoregressive coefficient on monthly unemployment falling to 0.776 (t-statistic 7.89) for the period 1978:6–1988:3 (i.e. June 1978–March 1988) when such policy variables are included, compared with a coefficient of 0.904 (t-statistic 9.31) in a richer dynamic model (Table 1, p. 807) without inclusion of the UI policy parameters. The authors note that this point estimate of 0.776 is very close to the figure of 0.780 (t-statistic 8.97) found for the period 1966:7–1978:5 in the model without policy variables, suggesting that the policy controls are responsible for the apparent increase in persistence after 1978. Furthermore, a dynamic simulation of unemployment that uses actual output figures and allows for feedback from the forecast unemployment rate in one year to the benefit eligibility figure for the next tracks the actual time-path of unemployment quite closely, while the same model without the policy-induced feedback overestimates unemployment prior to 1982 and seriously underestimates it thereafter.

Two sets of issues are raised by Milbourne, Purvis, and Scoones (1991), one narrow and one broad. The narrow issues involve assessment of the ability of their literal model to explain observed patterns of unemployment, both microeconomically and at the macroeconomic level, and on both of these narrow counts the verdict must be largely negative. Spells of unemployment in fact have many different lengths, with the mean duration of UI claims being systematically below the maximum eligibility period, contrary to the exact predictions of the microeconomic model. On a broader interpretation, however, the issue is more complex, though my judgment is that the balance of evidence is against such a large role for the UI system.

Card and Riddell (1993) provide two pieces of pertinent evidence. First, they use the (fixed) population of the persons reported as unemployed in the 1987 Labour Force Survey (Survey of Consumer Finances) and examine individual reported employment histories for the preceding year to determine weeks of work for qualification for UI benefits. Based on unemployment rates by labour-market region, they then calculate each individual's maximum number of weeks of eligibility for June of each year for the period 1972–89, and they aggregate these figures over regions using 1981 population weights. The resulting series (plotted in their Figure 5.13, p. 183) is compared with data for the average actual UI claim. These series are fairly similar in movement until the mid-1980s, though the levels differ markedly: while the average claim had a duration of about 21 weeks in 1983, for example, the maximum eligibility figure for that year was about 48 weeks, by this calculation. Since 1985, however, there has been a clear decline in the eligibility figure, tracking the overall decline in the unemployment rate nationally (and in most regions), while the duration of claims remained at over 18 weeks into 1989. This divergence suggests that, if the policy parameters substantially affected incidence or duration in the early 1980s, their role was much diminished by the end of the decade.[32]

The second piece of salient evidence comes from Card and Riddell's (1993) evidence on unemployed persons' employment patterns in the preceding year. For men, they find that the increase in non-employment time reported as unemployed (as opposed to reported as out of the labour force) is large among those with 0, 10, and 12 weeks of employment in the preceding year. For women, this growth is more even across employment experiences, but with some bunching at 10–12 weeks and at 20 weeks. Clearly, the 10- and 12-week concentrations for both sexes and the 20-week peak for women are probably in part responses to the UI system (including, for women, maternity-benefit entrance requirements), but the bunching at zero weeks of employment is more problematic for an explanation based on UI. Figures on relative recipiency rates between Canada and the United States (184) indicate that, for people with zero weeks of work, recipiency fell in Canada in the 1980s. Since this group accounts for a large part of the growth in unemployment, it is hard to interpret this as a consequence of greater UI generosity.

Corak and Jones (1993) examine the role of regional extended benefits directly by using administrative data from the Canadian UI program. They document the numbers of UI claimants in the regional extended benefit phase of a claim and examine how these numbers vary with the recession of the 1980s. As a proportion of all claimants in a year, recipients of regional extended benefits amounted to 18.5 per cent in 1978 and peaked at 28.1 per cent in 1984 before declining to 24.1 per cent by 1989 (Table 1, p. 15). Alternatively put, had the count of claimants remained at its 1981 level throughout the decade, the unemployment rate would have been 0.8, 1.6, and 1.2 percentage points lower in 1982, 1983, and 1984, respectively – figures that, while not insignificant, do not lead to the conclusion that regional benefits were the primary or direct mechanism behind the persistence of the early 1980s. Moreover, the authors' study of the time-series properties of the counts of recipients of regional extended benefits suggests no greater persistence in these series than in unemployment overall. They conclude that evidence from the administrative record goes against the view that the 1977 changes produced any direct effect capable of explaining the increased persistence of Canadian unemployment in the 1980s. Indirect effects (as from the potential length of UI benefits to the number of overall claims) would have to be particularly strong for the 1977 changes to have had any major role.[33]

Finally, in recent preliminary work, Gross (n.d.) has used flow data on Canadian UI recipients[34] to estimate a three-equation system determining inflows to UI recipiency, outflows from UI recipiency, and the relative cost of labour.[35] She argues, following Milbourne, Purvis, and Scoones, for increased persistence in both UI flows as a result of the 1977 changes, as well as for a central role for high energy prices and mismatch between workers' skills and employers' needs. Though her results depend on a number of special definitions of variables[36] and on a particular dynamic, econometric specification (p. 11), both of the estimated flow equations have a coefficient on the lagged-dependent variable that is significantly less than one. On these flow-based results, hysteresis would therefore be rejected.

LONG-TERM UNEMPLOYMENT AND DURATION DEPENDENCE

A final empirical issue addressed in some microeconometric Canadian work is the role of state-dependence in unemployment. In much recent research, inspired by Layard and others' studies of the United Kingdom, attention has turned to the distinctive role of long-term unemployment. I first review descriptive work on long-term unemployment in Canada. I then assess the importance of such evidence in the light of work on true and spurious duration dependence in unemployment.

Gera and McMullen (1991) and Rahman and Gera (1991) document the marked increase in the long-term unemployed as a proportion of the total unemployed pool in the 1980s. In 1976–79, given an average national unemployment rate of 7.6 per cent, nearly 15 per cent of those currently unemployed had been so for more than six months. By 1988–89, when the national average rate was similarly 7.6 per cent, the proportion with an elapsed spell in excess of six months was over 20 per cent. For interrupted durations of over one year in these two periods, the corresponding proportions were 3.6 per cent and 6.9 per cent, respectively (Gera and McMullen, 1991, Table 1.3, p. 6). Clearly, long-term unemployment has become more common.

From an international perspective, however, the incidence of long-term unemployment in Canada remains low. While the United States in the 1980s had a similar proportion of people unemployed over one year, many European economies had much higher rates, often correlated with higher unemployment. In 1986–88, in the United Kingdom, for example, the proportion stood at over 40 per cent, with a national unemployment rate of 10.6 per cent, while even in West Germany, with unemployment at 8.0 per cent, the proportion was 32 per cent (Rahman and Gera, 1991, Table 8.4, p. 103). Though the Canadian figures increased markedly in the 1980s, the performance still does not appear poor in comparative terms.

Rahman and Gera also present some preliminary evidence on correlates of long-term unemployment. First, they estimate a logistic model of the conditional probability of long-term unemployment, using data from the 1986 annual Labour Market Activity Survey. Though these data are not wholly satisfactory for the study of unemployment durations,[37] they will capture all long-term spells of continuous unemployment that, without interruption, either terminate in a job or are ongoing at the end of the calendar year 1986. The main findings are that the probability of long-term unemployment rises with age and is higher east of Ontario and in British Columbia. Rahman and Gera also discuss data on average exit probabilities,[38] which vary by region, by age, and by year in the period 1976–89. However, they do not attempt to estimate an econometric model of the determinants of unemployment durations, which would allow the individual's exit probability to vary with (elapsed) duration, as well as with a variety of observed covariates. Accordingly, it is hard to know exactly how the aggregate movement of these exit rates breaks down into individual dependence effects and compositional factors.

More fundamental, it remains difficult to distinguish unobserved heterogeneity and true duration dependence. The key problem is that, without such dependence, a researcher would still expect to find declining exit rates, provided that there is some heterogeneity in job-finding abilities that is not perfectly observed. Good job-finders will naturally tend to exit more quickly than those with poorer search abilities, leading to a declining observed pattern of exit rates, even conditional on observables such as education and demographics. However, this can hold in a model where, in fact, there is no genuine duration dependence (for example, where each person has a constant probability of leaving unemployment).[39] Alternatively, such an empirical pattern can also be generated by a population where each person faces a decline in the exit rate as the spell progresses – true duration dependence – but where, at any given duration of the elapsed spell of unemployment, the conditional exit probability is constant for all individuals.

Ham and Rea (1987) tackle these issues using 1975–80 data on men drawn from the Longitudinal Labour Force File from Employment and Immigration Canada. They deal with two forms of potential duration dependence in male unemployment. First, holding entitlement to UI benefits constant, they find (true) duration dependence induced by a variety of unobserved factors, such as changes in the intensity of job search with duration, in perceived wage-offer distribution, and in the degree to which financial-liquidity constraints are binding. Second, even ignoring these factors, duration dependence will be generated by the UI program, with fewer weeks of eligibility remaining as an unemployment spell lengthens and, as a consequence, the expectation that such a worker may be increasingly willing to investigate and accept poorer-quality jobs. The most significant difference between these two types of duration dependence from an empirical perspective is, of course, that an individual's remaining eligibility is in principle observable (or at least, can be imputed based on work history and the parameters of the benefit system), whereas other factors that might induce duration dependence may often be less easy to observe and quantify.

We should interpret Ham and Rea's results with caution in view of some limitations in their data. In particular, they have little demographic information, and, except for the earliest part of their sample period, wages are censored at the insured maximum value under the UI system (which means that wages above the maximum are only known to be at or above the maximum insurable figure). This latter problem is serious, as they note, since observations of wages above the insurable maximum lead to important independent variation in wages and benefits, and, without such data, the past wage (which can proxy for a parameter of the individual's perceived offer-distribution or for other aspects of unobserved heterogeneity) may be highly collinear with benefits. None the less, the findings reveal two aspects of duration dependence. First, potential exhaustion of UI benefits seems to play an important role, with the hazard (the transition rate out of unemployment into employment, conditional on having been unemployed up to that point) out of unemployment into employment turning up around 24 weeks in a number of alternative specifications. Second, apart from this "entitlement effect," the hazard tends to decline with duration, even when allowance is made along Heckman and

Singer's (1984) lines for unobserved heterogeneity. Overall, the effect is made up of these two contributions, with a number of model specifications suggesting (see their Figure 4, p. 350) that – with due allowance for heterogeneity and for varying entitlement with duration – the hazard clearly declines in the early weeks; it is probably almost constant for much of the interval between 10 weeks and 40 weeks; and the point estimate of the hazard seems to turn up at the longest durations, though here the sample is small and the upturn probably insignificant.[40]

Belzil (1990) also uses data from Employment and Immigration Canada's Longitudinal File – in this case, from January 1972 until December 1984. Though the details of Belzil's modelling and estimation differ from Ham and Rea's, it is more significant that he addresses a longer time perspective than they do. First, estimated UI effects persist beyond the current stretch of unemployment, principally by altering the quality of the employment match a worker achieves and thereby enabling more lasting employment to be found. Second, given this effect, there is no further evidence of lagged duration dependence: except for the benefit effect, additional weeks of unemployment do not materially alter the probability of leaving subsequent employment. With allowance for the causation through entitlements, then, Belzil's evidence is not inconsistent with a stationary search environment.

There are three other studies that should be discussed.[41] Osberg (1993) uses Labour Force Survey information from 1981, 1983, and 1986 to study the probability of transition from unemployment in January of each year to employment in February of the same year. Addressing duration dependence in terms of elapsed time since the previous job, Osberg's logistic estimates of the transition probability suggest that, for both men and women, negative duration dependence obtains for the short-term (three months or less) unemployed in 1983 and 1986, though for 1981 – where his sample antedates the real onset of the recession in that year – he is unable to reject the null hypothesis of stationarity. However, consistently across the three sample years, elapsed duration does not significantly affect the probability that a long-term unemployed person, defined as someone with a spell of more than three months, transits into employment. His interpretation (360) is that the former apparent decline in the hazard reflects "sorting," whereby unobserved heterogeneity sorts the unemployed, and that this is hence preferred to the "scarring" hypothesis, which in terms of the above discussion amounts to genuine duration dependence.

Preston, Saiyed, and Burns (1992) extend the Canadian study of the consequences of long-term unemployment using an age-based cohort model of the natural rate. By assumption, in this framework, the natural rate of unemployment for a cohort is determined by three factors: the unemployment rate of those of the same age one year previous; their own rate one year previous; and their own rate when they first entered the labour force. The authors show, given this model, that the aggregate natural rate can display considerable long-lived persistence, with scarring effects that literally last a lifetime, and they illustrate these results with a number of simulations. However, their initial assumption – that the cohort effects are so persistent as to encompass even the third element – is problematic. As we saw above, testing of this assumption (with US data, primarily) has not produced strong evidence in favour of such scarring and no evidence of the sort is presented for Canada.

Finally, Corak (1991b; 1993a; 1993c) exploits the UI records to document the nature of repeat use of the benefit system and to estimate various models of the determinants of such repetition. Beginning with spells in 1971 recorded following the UI act of that year, Corak denotes subsequent spells for an individual by a "sequence number" and demonstrates that, by the time the overall system appears to be in some sort of steady state (with regard to repeat usage), most spells are not the first one: in 1985, for example, about 40 per cent of male spells have a sequence number of 5 or higher, while the figure for women is closer to 20 per cent. Alternatively viewed, first spells are only about 20 per cent of all UI claims for both sexes in 1989. Clearly, the system involves a high degree of repeat use.

Corak addresses the determinants of such patterns in two ways. First, he uses Stern's (1986) method of logistic modelling of the probability that a given spell is followed by another within a specified period – specifically, that a claim is followed by another within 6 or 12 months. The results suggest strong seasonal factors, industry effects, and some influence from age. Further, measures of previous claims are important, with the probability of repetition within 14 weeks being 4 percentage points higher for a man on a second claim than for an otherwise identical man on a first claim. A similar effect is found for women, though the magnitude is somewhat smaller, at 2.5 percentage points (Corak 1991b, 26).

Second, Corak investigates Heckman and Borjas's (1980) notion of occurrence dependence, whereby past spells (of whatever length) influence the duration of current unemployment. Though a test for such dependence might be straightforward in a stationary environment, so that testing for mean occurrence dependence just amounts to a test for a difference in mean durations, according to the sequence number of the spell, in a changing economy the test must be performed conditional on observables. The criterion then amounts to whether the estimated parameter vector differs significantly for spells with different sequence numbers. The results stressed in Corak (1991b) concern the young, for whom the first sequence number probably is indeed the first actual spell, and the difference between the estimated determinants of the first and second spells. This focus of the first two spells stems from a belief that the habit or informational factors that could induce true occurrence dependence take effect quite quickly. The main finding is some evidence of occurrence dependence, with successive claims tending to become longer. For young men, the estimated mean duration of a second claim is 16 per cent higher than that of a first claim (39), while for young women, the increase is yet larger.

Overall, in an evaluation of the role of these various patterns of usage of the UI system, we should keep one idea in mind. Even in the absence of any true state dependence (whether duration dependence, occurrence dependence, or lagged duration dependence), one would expect repeat use of a benefit system, since many of the factors specific to the person or to their economic circumstances that cause a person to become a program participant initially will recur. Exactly how much repetition should be expected from what Corak terms this "neoclassical model" is much harder to quantify, but evidence of considerable repeat use does not per se imply state dependence. Corak (1991b; 1993a; 1993c) explains that his approach cannot distinguish between these two models.

In addition, it may be unclear whether adequate controls are present for all other institutional developments in the Canadian labour market since 1971. It may also be difficult to disentangle time effects – associated with macroeconomic conditions in a particular year, as well as with then-current legislation – from effects associated with the ageing of a particular cohort. Finally, it is hard to know the extent to which repeat users are drawn from those who might otherwise be employed, as opposed to being drawn into the labour force from a pool of people that would otherwise be non-participants in the labour force. Mortensen's "entitlement" effect of UI benefits may operate to make the latter source of program participants the larger, which may of course modify the interpretation of repeat use, whether or not it is associated with genuine state dependence. Overall, though, as a result of these problems of which the author is aware, it is hard to determine the extent of true state dependence in usage of the UI program.

One final issue pertinent to the entitlement effect of UI, as well as to Canadian-US divergence of experience in the 1980s, is the relative behaviour of the three labour-market stocks – employment, unemployment, and being out of the labour force. Card and Riddell (1993) note that, evaluated by the ratio of the stock of employed to the population as a whole, the labour-market performance of the two nations does not diverge sharply in the 1980s. In 1990, for example, the employment:population ratio stood at 62.7 per cent in the United States and at 61.5 per cent in Canada, both ratios having grown from the respective 1980 figures of 59.2 per cent and 59.3 per cent (1993, Table 5.1, p. 152). Average numbers of weeks of labour supply are also similar in the two countries.

These observations lead Card and Riddell to address the time-series behaviour of the mean probability of unemployment – given that the person concerned is not employed – which they term $P(U|N)$. For women, the relative rise in this conditional probability in the late 1970s explains the divergence between the two economies. For men, the rise is sharp for 1975–79, followed by a decline at the start of the 1980s and a subsequent continued climb until 1984. Again, the change in this probability is of the right order of magnitude to account for much of the relative behaviour of the two nations' unemployment rates, with a notably large contribution coming from unemployed men who had no reported weeks of work in the preceding year.

There seems to have been a change in the breakdown of the two non-employment states from the mid-1970s to the present that must in some way be related to the UI system. Despite some evidence of grouping of annual weeks of work around the points induced by the benefit system, the large part played by persons with low rates of receiving UI benefits in the overall rise of the unemployment rate must undermine any straightforward inculpation of the Canadian benefit system. Finally, an interesting issue that Card and Riddell raise is whether the increased likelihood that a non-employed person is counted as unemployed stems more from reduced work by people who would otherwise be employed or from increased claims from persons who would otherwise be non-participants.

CONCLUSION

This review of the main elements of empirical evidence concerning hysteresis in Canada has studied four areas of inquiry. First, there is a body of macroeconomic research on the determinants of inflation and unemployment – studying the Phillips curve, in essence – that I regard as the core of the standard debate on hysteresis and its implications for the conduct of economic policy. Results are fairly unambiguous in their rejection of hysteresis, with the clear exception of Fortin's recent work. There remains, however, debate about a variety of issues, including modelling of inflationary expectations, linearity of the Phillips curve, determination of potential output, and appropriate characterization of labour-market conditions. We return to some of this debate in the next chapter.

Second, and related, a number of papers have extended modelling of Canada's natural rate of unemployment. Though this literature has almost merged with that on the Phillips curve, and though the majority of these papers do not explicitly tackle how hysteresis (rather than persistence) would alter their conclusions, this work shows that the confidence intervals around estimates of the natural rate remain quite wide. We do not know the natural rate with any very useful precision.

The two other elements of this review of Canadian evidence were more microeconomic in nature, preparatory to the microeconometric examination below in chapter 6. Third, one very influential analysis of the apparently growing persistence in the Canadian unemployment rate in the 1980s is Milbourne, Purvis, and Scoones (1991). Their proposal was that the feedbacks in regional UI benefits could have induced strong persistence or even hysteresis. Several related studies have followed up on their suggestion, finding that while the sign of the effect is surely as they proposed, there is little evidence that the magnitude of this feedback is large enough to have played a substantial part. Fourth, I also surveyed some key work in the microeconometric study of duration dependence in Canadian unemployment spells, the idea being that such dependence – whereby the longer-term unemployed find it harder and harder to get jobs – could provide a robust microfoundation for hysteresis in the aggregate. Some of this research naturally overlaps with the studies of the UI system, though the attention to disentangling heterogeneity and true duration dependence is a hallmark of the microeconometric work. In sum, there are significant elements of dependence in the rate of escape from unemployment, some of which may be related to aspects of the UI legislation. We return to these issues below, in chapter 6.

5 Macroeconomics of Hysteresis in Canada

In this chapter, I examine macroeconomic work on the modelling of hysteresis and various approaches to testing. I first discuss univariate testing of the time-series properties of Canadian unemployment rates. Though such tests suggest non-stationarity, at least for some specifications, serious doubts must remain about the informativeness of this characterization for the rate of unemployment. I next consider the robustness of various attempts at estimation of an empirical Phillips curve. The main finding is that results indicative of hysteresis are rather sensitive to minor details of the econometric specification, raising questions about their general validity.

UNIVARIATE TIME-SERIES ANALYSIS

The first area of macroeconomic investigation that I pursue is the time-series properties of Canadian unemployment. I examine two series: the national rate of unemployment (CANSIM D767289) and the rate for men aged 25–54 (CANSIM D767404). Because some recent research suggests that standard seasonal-adjustment procedures (such as Census X-11) may distort the results from univariate test procedures (Ghysels 1988; 1990), I use both series in their seasonally unadjusted form.[1] Of course, for many purposes, the greatest interest will be in results using annual data, where such seasonality does not apply.

The standard procedure for testing for unit-root properties involves estimation of

$$y_t = \alpha + \beta t + \phi y_{t-1} + \sum_{j=0}^{k} \Delta y_{t-j}, \qquad (5.1)$$

where α is a constant, β the coefficient on a trend term, and k the number of included lags of the series (see, for example, Hamilton 1994, Table 17.3, pp. 528–9). Such an equation can be estimated by ordinary least squares, but inference for the estimated autoregressive parameter ϕ must recognize that, under the null hypothesis of a unit root, its distribution is non-standard. Accordingly, significance is assessed using the Dickey-Fuller tabulations (Fuller 1976, 371 and 373), based on Monte Carlo evaluation of the distribution; these critical values naturally depend on sample size. Furthermore, the appropriate level of significance depends on whether or not the estimated equation includes an intercept and/or a time trend. Finally, the results will depend on inclusion of the correct number of lags in the final term of the equation, with too few altering the size of the test and too many lowering the power of the test against a stationary alternative.

Table 5.1 gives the results in various cases with a constant term, with and without trends, and with varying specifications of the number of lagged changes included in the equation. In each case, the test statistic is given; it may be compared with the critical values given in the lower part of the table. For the annual data, both the national unemployment rate and the rate for prime-age males reject a unit root only when a trend is included and there is exactly one lagged value in the equation. This integration of order one matches the results of Atkins, Bruce, and King (1991, 12). In contrast, for the monthly data, the general pattern of test statistics rejects the unit-root hypothesis in favour of a stationary alternative, whether or not a trend is included, and with little variation across different lag specifications. Our interpretation of this difference is that the monthly data, which are not seasonally adjusted, contain a good deal of extraneous noise that confounds the unit-root test and that, as a consequence, the results from annual data are to be preferred.

There are a number of statistical and econometric issues that arise in use of these Dickey-Fuller tests, and a large literature

Table 5.1
Dickey-Fuller univariate tests

	Annual		*Monthly*	
	Unemp	*U male*	*Unemp*	*U male*
0 lags, no trend	–1.08	–1.02	–2.46	–3.17*
0 lags, trend	–1.98	–2.27	–3.84*	–4.18**
1 lag, no trend	–1.48	–1.47	–3.68**	–5.65**
1 lag, trend	–3.15*	–3.39*	–5.71**	–7.22**
2 lags, no trend	–1.40	–1.31	–4.23**	–7.06**
2 lags, trend	–2.79	–2.93	–6.68**	–9.27**
3 lags, no trend	–1.09	–0.90	–3.31*	–5.16**
3 lags, trend	–2.63	–2.79	–5.34**	–6.99**
4 lags, no trend	–1.04	–0.79	–2.61	–7.33**
4 lags, trend	–2.26	–2.55	–4.14**	–4.58**

Critical values

	N = 25		*N* = 500	
Level of test	0.05	0.01	0.05	0.01
Trend	–3.00	–3.75	–2.87	–3.44
No trend	–3.60	–4.38	–3.42	–3.98

Notes: Annual data 1960–90, monthly data 1954:1–1991:1.
* and ** denote statistical significance at the 5 per cent and 1 per cent levels, respectively.

attempts to generalize the results. While this is clearly not the place to survey this voluminous work,[2] analogous testing procedures now available allow for the driving innovations to be weakly dependent (rather than serially independent, as in the Dickey-Fuller approach) and permit such innovations to have heterogeneous distributions (rather than the homoskedasticity previously required). In particular, Phillips and Perron (1988) develop two statistics, Z_α and Z_t, transformations of, respectively, the standardized estimator and the *t*-statistic from the regression, which have invariant limiting distributions for a wide class of weakly dependent and heterogeneously distributed innovation series (see, for example, Hamilton 1994, Table 17.2, p. 514). I have accordingly also implemented these newer tests on the same annual and monthly data for unemployment overall and among prime-age males (Table 5.2).

The pattern of results for these Phillips-Perron tests is similar to that for the Dickey-Fuller procedures, with the annual series failing to reject a unit root no matter what the lag specification, while the

Table 5.2
Phillips-Perron univariate tests

	Annual		*Monthly*	
	Unemp	*U male*	*Unemp*	*U male*
Z_t, 0 lags	−1.12	−1.05	−2.46	−3.18*
Z_t, 1 lag	−1.28	−1.25	−2.93*	−3.96**
Z_t, 2 lags	−1.34	−1.32	−3.24*	−4.51**
Z_t, 3 lags	−1.32	−1.31	−3.34*	−4.73**
Z_t, 4 lags	−1.28	−1.27	−3.28*	−4.69**
Z_α, 0 lags	−2.49	−2.54	−13.18	−22.21**
Z_α, 1 lag	−3.28	−3.45	−18.24*	−33.46**
Z_α, 2 lags	−3.58	−3.84	−22.09**	−42.71**
Z_α, 3 lags	−3.50	−3.79	−23.34**	−46.87**
Z_α, 4 lags	−3.28	−3.58	−22.54**	−46.13**

Critical values

	N = 25		*N = 500*	
Level of test	0.05	0.01	0.05	0.01
Z_t statistic	−3.00	−3.75	−2.87	−3.44
Z_α statistic	−12.5	−17.2	−14.0	−20.5

Notes: Annual data 1960–90, monthly data 1954:1–1991:1.
* and ** denote statistical significance at the 5 per cent and 1 per cent levels, respectively.

monthly data reject in almost all cases. Again, the annual results seem more important, given the evident seasonality in the higher-frequency data.

Thus these results seem to suggest unit-root behaviour in both the national and the prime-age–male rates, especially using the annual data for the past three decades. Are these results sensible, and do they imply the presence of hysteresis?

In any finite sample, it is hard to distinguish between a stationary series with a high degree of persistence and a (non-stationary) series with a unit root. The key differentiating factor is their behaviour in the long term, when the stationary series returns to its long-run mean while the unit-root series displays no such reversion. Likely behaviour of the series over the long haul becomes crucial, and, given this fact, characterization of the unemployment rate as a linear process with a unit root is not sensible. The rate of unemployment will not even begin to approach either natural boundary – namely, 0 and 1 – so the linear non-stationary model cannot be correct. Rather, it is more probable that the rate will remain around the range experienced in the past 30 years, with potentially long-lived and persistent deviations away from this mean. Accordingly, the preferred interpretation mirrors Cochrane (1991, 207–8), which denies the informativeness of unit-root testing for most macroeconomic series. To reconcile this view with the findings in the two tables above, one can posit that it results from imposing a linear structure on a globally non-linear process. Alternatively, as already noted, on the basis of a short span of data, it is exceedingly difficult to distinguish between a persistent but stationary series and one with a genuine unit root.

Finally, fractional differencing offers an alternative framework for analysis of the univariate properties of a series such as GDP or unemployment (Granger and Joyeux 1980; Hosking 1981; Diebold and Rudebusch 1989). Generalizing the idea of an autoregressive integrated moving-average model (ARIMA), the fractional integrated model (ARFIMA) for a series X_t in terms of innovations e_t can be written as

$$a(L)\ (1 - L)^d\ X_t = b(L)\ e_t$$

where $a(L)$ and $b(L)$ are polynomials in the lag operator L and where, unlike the standard ARIMA case, the parameter d can be a real number.[3] In the stationary (ARMA) model $d = 0$, and in the standard ARIMA model $d = 1$. This ARFIMA model for X_t has d lying between –0.5 and 0.5 for stationary and invertibility, though one can, by letting $Y_t = (1 - L)\ X_t$ be its first difference, generalize to values of d between 0.5 and 1.5 if Y_t itself obeys an ARFIMA process. The long-run properties of a fractionally differenced series depend on the value of d, with a value less than 1 leading to shocks having only temporary effects, though even in this case the ARFIMA model will display long-lived response to a disturbance.[4]

The only application to Canadian evidence of the ARFIMA model of which I am aware is an unpublished paper by Koustas and Veloce (1993). They estimate such a model using a two-step procedure, first finding the parameter d spectrally and then estimating the elements of the polynomials $a(L)$ and $b(L)$ on the transformed series, and they report results on quarterly data for output per head and the unemployment rate overall and for three demographic groups. For their preferred specification, they find estimates of d of 0.92 for real GDP per capita (1947:Q1–1992:Q4) and 0.89 for unemployment (1953:Q1–1992:Q4). The ranking of the demographic groups from highest to lowest persistence of unemployment rates is men over 25, women over 25, and youth.[5] The implied values for the permanent component of the unemployment rate match this ranking of the three groups (1993, 16).

In quantitative terms, the importance of the ARFIMA approach can best be appreciated by consideration of the cumulative-impulse response functions that Koustas and Veloce generate based on their ARMA estimation using the *d*-transformed data.[6] For real output per head, a one per cent shock has 0.943 of its original effect after one hundred years, while for unemployment, such a shock has 0.633 of its initial size after a similar lag! Clearly, while *d* is less than one, so that the effect is indeed temporary in the long run, this is an instance where Keynes's maxim "In the long run we are all dead" is appropriate. However, the standard errors for these figures are likely to be quite large: for the initial estimates of *d* – the integration parameter – the standard errors were about 0.25 in both cases. Such problems reflect the difficulty of estimating long-memory models on a relatively short span of data, though Koustas and Veloce note (1993, 22) that a multivariate approach of fractional cointegration may increase the efficiency of estimation.[7]

Overall, with regard to the hysteresis question, there remains some doubt about the significance of the univariate results. In a finite sample, certainly, there need be no link between the univariate unit-root test results and the types of multivariate analysis – for or against the idea of hysteresis – pursued below. It is not clear how useful the univariate modelling is for the key issues of economic importance.

EMPIRICAL PHILLIPS CURVES: ROBUSTNESS

As discussed in the review of past work in the earlier chapters, the leading framework for analysis of hysteresis is the standard empirical Phillips curve. Here I give a brief exposition of this work and assess the robustness of recent Canadian empirical findings in this area.

The starting point is an expectations-augmented Phillips curve of the form

$$\pi_t = a\pi_{t-1} + b(u_t - u_t^*), \tag{5.2}$$

where π_t is the rate of inflation, u_t the rate of unemployment, and u_t^* the "natural" rate of unemployment, all as of period t. The first term in (5.2) proxies inflationary expectations and can include a number of lagged-inflation terms; under some conditions, often termed the "accelerationist restriction," the sum of the coefficients of these lagged terms will equal unity. In this context, the novelty of a hysteresis viewpoint is that the current "natural" rate may depend not only on structural and demographic variables, here termed x_t (with a coefficient vector γ), but also on the past value of the unemployment rate itself:

$$u_t^* = hu_{t-1} + \gamma x_t. \tag{5.3}$$

As a result, substitution of (5.3) into (5.2) yields

$$\begin{aligned}\pi_t &= a\pi_{t-1} + b(u_t + hu_{t-1} - \gamma x_t)\\ &= a\pi_{t-1} + b(1 - h)\, u_t + bh(u_t - u_{t-1}) - b\gamma x_t,\end{aligned} \tag{5.4}$$

so that hysteresis obtains with $h = 1$ when the level of unemployment does not enter significantly into such an estimated Phillips curve but when the change of the rate is significant.[8]

Depending on the issue being addressed, the key question is whether or not there is "full" hysteresis – that is, whether or not $h = 1$. To see this, consider the calculation of the so-called "sacrifice ratio" – the (undiscounted) amount of temporary unemployment (or output loss, depending on the specification) associated with a permanent reduction of one percentage point in the rate of inflation.[9] In the simple case when $a = 1$ in equation (5.2), equation (5.4) yields

$$\frac{\partial \pi}{\partial u} = b(1 - h) + bh = b, \tag{5.5}$$

and, one period ahead,

$$\frac{\partial \pi_{+1}}{\partial u} = \frac{\partial \pi}{\partial u} - bh = b(1 - h), \tag{5.6}$$

with the same effect for inflation rates in all subsequent periods. The sacrifice ratio is given by the reciprocal of this long-run effect –

$$\frac{1}{b(1-h)}, \tag{5.7}$$

and it thus depends *only* on the level coefficient in (5.4), not on the change term. This result is quite general and continues to hold if the one lagged value of inflation in (5.2) is replaced by a distributed lag of arbitrary length and if more lagged values of unemployment enter on the right-hand side of the equation.[10] For this issue, at least, it follows that a salient result from the perspective of hysteresis must have both the change of unemployment significant and the level effect insignificant. If both the level and the change play a role in the determination of inflation, given inflationary expectations, the sacrifice ratio depends on the level coefficient alone.[11]

As detailed in the preceding chapter, two recent studies have adopted similar approaches to the measurement of hysteresis in Canadian labour markets, with rather opposing results. Cozier and Wilkinson (1991) estimated a particular variant of (5.4) using either an output gap or an unemployment gap, according to the specification. Imposing the so-called accelerationist restriction – that the sum of all coefficients on lagged values of inflation equal unity in (2) – they reach the particular specification

$$\begin{aligned}\Delta\pi_t = a &+ \sum_{i=1}^{4} \beta_i \Delta\pi_{t-i} + \delta_1 YGAP_{t-1} + \delta_2 \Delta YGAP_{t-1} \\ &+ b\Delta AIB + \sum_{i=0}^{4} c_i \Delta PCOM_{t-i} \\ &+ \sum_{i=0}^{1} d_i \Delta POIL_{t-i} + e, \qquad (5.8)\end{aligned}$$

with

$$\beta_i = -\sum_{j=i+1}^{k} \alpha_j, \qquad (5.9)$$

where the α_j terms are the coefficients of the k-distributed lags on past inflation in their variant of (5.2).

Estimated using quarterly data from 1964:Q3 to 1988:Q4, their broad finding is against hysteresis. In the case of unemployment, they find that the level is significant and the change is not in (5.8), while for the output gap, both level and change exert positive, significant effects on the rate of inflation. However, if the interest lies in computation of the sacrifice ratio, which in this case is given by

$$\frac{1 - \sum_{i=1}^{k-1} \beta_i}{\delta_1}, \tag{5.10}$$

then only the level coefficient δ_1 matters, as in the earlier example.

In sharp contrast, Fortin (1991) examined Canadian evidence for hysteresis in unemployment, finding a strong case for hysteresis, at least in recent years. His basic empirical specification is

$$\begin{aligned} \pi_t = c + A\pi_{t-1} + B_1 u_t + B_2 \Delta u_t + B_3 \Delta u_{t-1} \\ + B_4 \Delta u_{t-2} + C_1 \, Food \, \pi_{t-1} + C_2 \, Energy \, \pi_{t-1} \\ + C_3 \, Imports \, \pi_t + C_4 \, Indirecttaxchange_t \\ + C_5 \, AIB, \end{aligned} \tag{5.11}$$

which estimates this Phillips curve in levels, not in the changes adopted by the preceding authors, and which allows for a number of lagged values of the change in the (male) unemployment rate. Use of the male unemployment rate is intended to minimize structural (principally demographic) changes that may have altered its natural rate and hence removes the need to model explicitly the x_t variables in (5.3). As noted in the preceding chapter, though Fortin's model yields relatively conventional results when estimated on annual data from 1957 to 1990, when he permits some variables (specifically the constant term, the level of the male unemployment rate, and the current and two lagged changes of this rate) to have different effects before and after 1973, the data in the more recent period suggest that the level is insignificant but that the change is significantly negative, as hysteresis would require.

Thus two recent studies have reached almost diametrically opposed conclusions.[12] The most fruitful way to proceed is therefore to assess the robustness of the results, examining alternative specifications, lag structures, break points, and so on to determine whether the results of interest hinge on some model specification in which one may have only marginal confidence. Such an investigation has been performed, and summary results are reported in Tables 5.3 and 5.4.

Table 5.3
Quarterly results, Cozier and Wilkinson's data

	Equation 1.2		*Equation 1.4*	
	UGAP	*DRNU*	*YGAP*	*DYGAP*
Basic specification	–0.33*	–1.12	0.27**	0.57*
	(0.14)	(0.66)	(0.11)	(0.26)
AR1 (CORC) error correction	–0.27*	–1.06+	0.20**	0.62**
	(0.11)	(0.55)	(0.08)	(0.21)
Sample 73:1–88:4 only	–0.32+	–1.29+	0.31*	0.17
	(0.17)	(0.76)	(0.13)	(0.37)
Seasonals added	–0.33*	–1.11+	0.27**	0.60*
	(0.14)	(0.66)	(0.10)	(0.26)
Level and change – 1 lag	–0.29*	–1.24+	–	–
	(0.14)	(0.67)		
Level and change – 1 lag	1.29	–2.47	0.22+	–0.43
	(1.67)	(1.89)	(0.11)	(0.28)
and 2 lags	–1.63	–0.65	–	0.70*
	(1.69)	(0.78)		(0.28)
Change lagged 0–1 quarters	–0.31*	–0.80	–	–
	(0.14)	(0.76)		
Change lagged 0–2 quarters	–0.30*	–0.80	0.25*	0.50+
	(0.14)	(0.76)	(0.11)	(0.27)
Change lagged 0–3 quarters	–0.29*	–0.76	0.25*	0.50+
	(0.14)	(0.76)	(0.11)	(0.27)
Change lagged 0–4 quarters	–0.30*	–0.62	0.22*	0.49+
	(0.14)	(0.77)	(0.11)	(0.27)
Use of RNU level and change	–0.16	–1.20+	–	–
	(0.10)	(0.67)		
Use of UGAP level and change	–0.32*	–0.74	–	–
	(0.14)	(0.61)		
Annual data: same lags	–0.75+	0.15	0.30	1.09*
	(0.40)	(0.91)	(0.35)	(0.54)
Annual data: "annual" lags	–0.60*	–0.68	0.28	0.48*
	(0.26)	(0.43)	(0.22)	(0.21)
Annual data: unemployment lagged 0–1	–0.64**	–0.27	0.28	0.48*
	(0.25)	(0.46)	(0.24)	(0.22)

+, *, and ** denote coefficients that are statistically different from zero at the 10 per cent, 5 per cent, and 1 per cent levels, respectively. Standard errors in parentheses.

Table 5.3 gives the coefficient and standard error on the level and change variables in question for Cozier and Wilkinson's model, first replicating their results, then considering a number of interesting alternatives. In particular, I allow for a different error structure, restrict the sample period to 1973 and later, add seasonal dummy variables, and alter the lag structure for either or both the level and the change of output or unemployment. While the results *do* differ for these alternatives, in a manner that clearly influences the estimated values of the sacrifice ratio (as computed from [5.10] using the estimates of β_i and δ_1), none produces a significant change and an insignificant level effect, as hysteresis would require. I also investigate use of the national unemployment rate (RNU in Cozier and Wilkinson) and its change, or use of the Bank of Canada's computed UGAP (a measure of the difference between the actual rate of unemployment and the Bank's estimate of the natural rate) and its change, with no difference in the results. Finally, I convert these quarterly data to an annual basis, and, for output but not for unemployment, some results supportive of hysteresis can be generated; these cells are shaded in the table.[13] Overall, though, the balance of Table 5.3 must be said to go against this view.

Table 5.4 performs a similar exercise using Fortin's model and data, and, again, cells that generate significance from the change but not the level are shaded. The first line reports the base specification, with the post-break figures in the final two columns being the main evidence for hysteresis. However, these results appear not to be robust to minor changes of modelling or econometrics. Allowance for fewer (than two) lags of the change in the male unemployment rate undermines the result, as does moving to a 1971 or 1972 break date (instead of 1973). Further, estimation without allowing a split in the sample produces no hysteretic results, though allowing both the level and the change of unemployment to have different coefficients before and after 1973 does not alter Fortin's principal result, provided that two lags of the change are included; indeed, all variables in the model can be split without losing the result, given the other details of the specification. However, as before, small changes in the lag structure undercut this finding quite sharply.[14]

One way of thinking about the magnitude of these various results in Tables 5.3 and 5.4 is to examine the implied value for the hysteresis parameter. Consider (5.4), where the coefficient on the level of unemployment is $b(1 - h)$ and the coefficient on the change in unemployment is bh. It follows that the ratio of the change coefficient to the sum of the change and level coefficients yields a point estimate of the hysteresis parameter h:

$$\frac{bh}{b(1-h)+bh} = h.$$

Table 5.4
Annual results, Fortin's Innis Lecture data

	Pre-break date		Post-break date	
	UMale1	*DUmale1*	*UMale2*	*DUmale2*
Basic specification	–0.42**	0.26+	–0.06	–0.38**
	(0.10)	(0.13)	(0.08)	(0.14)
Only 1 lag of DUMale2	–0.40**	0.24	–0.17*	–0.27+
	(0.11)	(0.15)	(0.08)	(0.15)
No lags of DUMale2	–0.54*	0.48+	–0.37*	0.07
	(0.22)	(0.29)	(0.16)	(0.28)
AR1 (CORC) error term	–0.38**	0.18	–0.06	–0.38**
	(0.10)	(0.15)	(0.08)	(0.14)
AR1, 1 DUMale2 lag	–0.35**	0.16	–0.16*	–0.24
	(0.11)	(0.16)	(0.08)	(0.15)
AR1, no DUMale2 lag	–0.54	0.31	–0.80**	0.41+
	(0.34)	(0.25)	(0.25)	(0.22)
1971 break	–0.43**	0.25+	–0.18*	–0.32*
	(0.11)	(0.15)	(0.07)	(0.16)
1971 break, 1 DUMale2 lag	–0.42**	0.25	–0.24**	–0.23
	(0.12)	(0.16)	(0.07)	(0.16)
1971 break, no DUMale2 lag	–0.57*	0.57*	–0.29*	0.15
	(0.22)	(0.29)	(0.13)	(0.28)
1972 break	–0.43**	0.27+	–0.14*	–0.34*
	(0.11)	(0.14)	(0.07)	(0.15)
1972 break, 1 DUMale2 lag	–0.42**	0.26+	–0.20**	–0.25
	(0.11)	(0.15)	(0.07)	(0.15)
1972 break, no DUMale2 lag	–0.55*	0.54+	–0.32*	–0.13
	(0.22)	(0.29)	(0.13)	(0.28)
1974 break	–0.42**	0.25+	–0.07	–0.38**
	(0.10)	(0.13)	(0.09)	(0.14)
1974 break, 1 DUMale2 lag	–0.41**	0.22	–0.21*	–0.29+
	(0.11)	(0.14)	(0.09)	(0.15)
1974 break, no DUMale2 lag	–0.55*	0.43	–0.43*	0.03
	(0.22)	(0.28)	(0.16)	(0.28)
1975 break	–0.44**	0.27*	–0.02	–0.39**
	(0.10)	(0.13)	(0.09)	(0.14)
1975 break, 1 DUMale2 lag	–0.43**	0.25+	–0.15	–0.28+
	(0.12)	(0.15)	(0.09)	(0.16)
1975 break, no DUMale2 lag	–0.58*	0.48+	–0.37*	0.03
	(0.22)	(0.28)	(0.16)	(0.28)

Applying this calculation to the results of Tables 5.3 and 5.4 produces a number of interesting results.

First, Cozier and Wilkinson's basic specification generates estimates of 0.77 (using unemployment) and 0.70 (using output), even though in both cases the level effect is clearly statistically significant. In contrast, Fortin's preferred model has a value of 0.87 in

Table 5.4
(continued)

	Price homogeneity		*No price homogeneity*	
	UMale	*DUmale*	*UMale*	*DUmale*
Basic specification	–0.06	–0.38**	–0.09	–0.32*
	(0.08)	(0.14)	(0.09)	(0.15)
No split	–0.16	–0.07	–0.15+	–0.07
	(0.08)	(0.16)	(0.08)	(0.17)
"Symmetric" splits	–0.05	–0.37*	–0.09	–0.28+
	(0.09)	(0.15)	(0.10)	(0.17)
All variables split: 1957–72	–0.50	0.21	–0.71**	0.39*
	(0.21)	(0.20)	(0.16)	(0.15)
1973 on	–0.10	–0.32**	–0.08	–0.36*
	(0.07)	(0.11)	(0.07)	(0.14)
Only 1 lag of DUMale				
Basic specification	–0.17*	–0.27+	–0.22*	–0.20
	(0.08)	(0.15)	(0.09)	(0.16)
No split	–0.19**	–0.02	–0.19*	–0.02
	(0.07)	(0.16)	(0.08)	(0.16)
"Symmetric" splits	–0.17*	–0.27+	–0.22*	–0.19
	(0.08)	(0.15)	(0.09)	(0.17)
All variables split: 1957–72	–0.36*	0.11	–0.47**	0.21
	(0.18)	(0.19)	(0.17)	(0.18)
1973 on	–0.21*	–0.22	–0.20*	–0.24
	(0.09)	(0.16)	(0.10)	(0.21)
No lags of DUMale				
Basic specification	–0.37*	–0.07	–0.48**	0.26
	(0.16)	(0.28)	(0.15)	(0.27)
No split	–0.23*	0.10	–0.22*	0.10
	(0.10)	(0.21)	(0.10)	(0.22)
"Symmetric" splits	–0.37*	0.07	–0.48**	–0.26
	(0.16)	(0.28)	(0.15)	(0.27)
All variables split: 1957–72	–0.37**	0.12	–0.40*	0.17
	(0.13)	(0.17)	(0.11)	(0.15)
1973 on	–0.35	0.23	–0.42*	0.46
	(0.22)	(0.39)	(0.21)	(0.38)

+, *, and ** denote coefficients that are statistically different from zero at the 10 per cent, 5 per cent, and 1 per cent levels, respectively. Standard errors in parentheses.

the post-1973 period but a negative value (of –1.63) before 1973, with the latter being a consequence of the opposing signs of his estimates of the level and change effects for the earlier period.

Second, regarding the sensitivity of Cozier and Wilkinson's specification, the results using unemployment (1.2) in Table 5.3 almost always produce a point estimate of between 0.6 and 0.8, even though in no case is the change effect significant and the level effect insignificant. The analogous output-based figures – in (1.4) – display somewhat more variation, and the three instances where hysteresis might be supported (using annual data) have values for *h* between 0.63 and 0.78.

Third, the alternative specifications of the Fortin model reported in Table 5.4 give rise to a large range of implied values for the hysteresis parameter. With the level and change effects on unemployment having different effects before and after a break date (1973 in Fortin's base model), all of the pre-break estimates are incorrectly signed; this is a consequence of the change effect for this period always having a positive estimated coefficient. After the break, the estimates of *h* are also quite varied. The highest value, 0.95, comes from the 1975 split date, with two lagged values of the change in unemployment, but there are many cases where the sign remains incorrect. Of the instances where the level and change coefficients are both negative, the values of *h* can fall as low as 0.49.

Finally, one can also examine a confidence interval around the hysteresis parameter, allowing for the fact that our estimates of the level and the change effects are not independent. Taking a first-order expansion and using the estimates of the variances of the level and change coefficients and their covariance, we can reach an expression for the (asymptotic) variance of the parameter *h* as

$$Var(h) = \frac{L^2 Var(C) + C^2 Var(L) - 2Cov(C, L)\,CL}{(C+L)^4},$$

where *L* denotes the estimated level coefficient, and *C* the estimated change coefficient.[15] Focusing on the instances where hysteresis appears to be supported in Tables 5.3 and 5.4 (i.e. the shaded cells), I find that the implied standard errors on the hysteresis parameter are usually quite large. In the annual results at the bottom of Table 5.3, the standard error is always about 0.25, while the point estimates range from 0.63 to 0.78; one cannot usually reject therefore the hypothesis that $h = 1.00$ at a 95 per cent confidence level. In the results in Table 5.4 that are supportive of hysteresis, the standard errors are typically a little smaller. For Fortin's preferred specification in the post-1973 period, the point estimate of 0.87 has a standard error (s.e.) of 0.18. This changes only slightly to 0.86 (s.e. 0.18) with AR1 errors, to 0.84 (s.e. 0.19) with a 1974 break, and to 0.95 (s.e. 0.21) with a 1975 break. Similar results also hold for the shaded cells in the second part of Table 5.4, where alternative sample splits are investigated and where price homogeneity is not imposed. Once again there is a wide confidence interval for each estimate of *h*.

Clearly, in view of these substantial standard errors around the point estimates of the hysteresis parameter, *h*, it would be unwise to make much (if anything) of minor differences in the estimates themselves. This lack of precision may affect the formulation of economic policy, though – a point to which I return below.

With regard to the few results in Table 5.4 that suggest some evidence of hysteresis, one informative mode of analysis is to envisage the microeconomic mechanisms that might give rise to such hysteresis, along some of the lines suggested by the theoretical work surveyed in chapter 2.[16] The central issue here seems to be the number of lagged values of unemployment, in the form of its level or its change, included in the empirical Phillips curve specification, with the broad-brush finding being that two annual lags are required, even after 1973, to generate hysteretic results.

For this result to have a microeconomic counterpart, one would require that de-skilling and scarring effects from long-term unemployment take effect after two years, or that some other mechanism operate, directly or indirectly, with a similar lag. However, as noted in chapter 4, Canadian long-term unemployment is not a large proportion of total unemployment, by international standards, and the number of unemployed persons with elapsed durations exceeding two years is very small. As a consequence, it is hard to believe that direct effects of such unemployment, operating through these small numbers of people, are enough to drive the effect of the overall national unemployment rate on the rate of inflation, as the empirical Phillips-curve specification might suggest. Rather, the conclusion is either that the process is quite indirect – perhaps operating through the wage-setting behaviour of the employed, in some manner yet to be specified, or through some sort of lagged duration dependence – or that the results with long lags of the level and change of unemployment may not truly be structural. My current tendency is to lean toward the latter position.

Overall, while the results in Tables 5.3 and 5.4 clearly are mixed, the evidence favouring hysteresis is less robust than that which disconfirms it.

Finally, some recent work by Poloz and Wilkinson (1992), conducted independently but simultaneously with the present inquiry, has similarly found that most of the results that support hysteresis are not robust, while the opposing evidence seems markedly less fragile. Poloz and Wilkinson in particular address Fortin (1991) and Cozier and Wilkinson (1991), especially from the perspective of alternative data sources, to assess the cause of their disagreement in results. Their study exactly complements my work that looks at alternative lag structures, error specifications, and break points.

The specific alternative versions of the two models that Poloz and Wilkinson examine include alternative measures of the natural rate or of potential output, both summarized as measuring "the gap," data frequency (annual or quarterly data), alternative measures of the rate of inflation, and the stability of the estimated equations over time. While their paper contains many results, not all of which can be detailed here, we should note the circumstances when they can clearly reject or confirm hysteresis. Rejections are obtained using Fortin's exact specification but employing many measures of the gap other than the rate of adult male unemployment; total unemployment rate, the unemployment rate adjusted for demographic trends,[17] the female unemployment rate, the youth unemployment rate, and the output gap all result in rejection of hysteresis, when each is entered into Fortin's equation.[18] Similarly, use of the (overall) consumer price index (CPI) or the GDP deflator, instead of the CPI net of food and energy, removes the inference of hysteresis in Fortin's model.

In contrast, fewer results support hysteresis. Fortin's result is consistent in annual data (which was the version he presented, of course) or in an analogous quarterly implementation, provided that the data sources used are male unemployment and CPI net of price changes in food and energy, while the only instance in Cozier and Wilkinson's results that generates hysteresis, in Poloz and Wilkinson's study of the data source permutations, is when adult female unemployment is used as the measure of the gap. Despite the annual version of Cozier and Wilkinson's results presented above in Table 5.3, Poloz and Wilkinson find no difference in the results when they address alternative data frequencies. This contrast hinges on lag structures, with their annual findings in Table 4 (1992, 13) using only contemporaneous measures of the level and the difference of the lag variable, in contrast to the single lagged value admitted in my Table 5.3, above.

It is perhaps not surprising, in view of the potential importance of the results, that the discrepancy between these two papers' findings on hysteresis should have provoked more than one study as to its cause. Accordingly, I find it striking that my work and that of Poloz and Wilkinson (1992) obtain such complementary and yet similar results. The results are complementary, since the methods of investigation have been quite different – with their detailed study of data sources, differences, and anomalies contrasting with my work on lag structures, error specifications, treatment of the break date, and so on. Yet the results are finally very similar, since, in both cases, the conclusion is reached that the evidence in favour of hysteresis is quite thin, while that against is relatively strong and robust.

CONCLUSION

The clear conclusion from the range of macroeconomic work performed and discussed in this chapter is that there is no strong evidence in favour of hysteresis in the Canadian labour market. Though the univariate modelling of the rate of unemployment did suggest a large, autoregressive parameter, this hint at hysteresis was emphatically not supported in the multivariate analysis. In particular, a variety of empirical Phillips curve specifications were estimated, with allowance for alternative structures of lagged variables and disturbance terms, alternative potential break points in the data, and so on, and the results in favour of hysteresis were seen not to be robust to a large number of small changes in modelling. The present conclusion in this regard was recently echoed in independent but complementary work discussed above at some length. Overall, then, the macroeconomic results are remarkably clear in their failure to find hysteresis in Canadian labour markets.

6 Microeconomic Foundations and Estimation

In this chapter, I employ individual-level data to extend existing analysis of unemployment persistence and hysteresis in a variety of directions. I use as my primary microeconomic data source the best available Canadian panel data – the Labour Market Activity Survey (LMAS) – which I introduce in the first section of this chapter. However, since serious problems have recently come to light regarding interpretation of the various non-employment states as coded in the LMAS, I match – in the second section – the LMAS to the monthly information on the labour market from the Labour Force Survey (LFS) for the six months that each LMAS subject was in the LFS sample. In the third section, I examine a two-state model – employment, and non-employment – a binary division unaffected by data problems associated with the LMAS. For both LMAS-LFS matching and the two-state model, a number of alternative, hazard-based models of the determinants of unemployment or non-employment duration are studied. The results show some patterns of duration dependence, but there is considerable variation across specifications and between the unemployment and the non-employment estimates. In the fourth section, in an attempt to assess the potential importance of the multiple-equilibria approach, I estimate a matching function using data on labour-market gross flows and a help-wanted index. The matching function results do not generally support one of the conditions usually associated with multiplicity. The fifth section is a brief conclusion.

DATA FOR THE MICROECONOMIC STUDY OF UNEMPLOYMENT

State dependence in unemployment may provide one microfoundation for hysteresis at the level of the macroeconomy. This subsection investigates a variety of models and estimates of hysteresis using individual-level data drawn primarily from the LMAS (Statistics Canada 1990), supplemented by some other data sources.

In using the LMAS to study unemployment duration and its determinants, researchers must confront the so-called LMAS filter, because the weekly information on non-employment states in the LMAS is "filtered" (Jones and Riddell 1995). The design of the LMAS questionnaire – which, except for special treatment of year-end, links all periods of non-employment to a subsequent job, and which records only unemployment spells that are continuous and that terminate in that job – excludes a potentially important number of unemployment spells. As a consequence, it does not seem that much can be usefully gained from an uncritical analysis of the unemployment spells produced from the LMAS.[1]

There are two promising avenues that can be followed, given this problem, and each is introduced here and investigated more in the next two sections of this chapter.

First, for each person in the LMAS, which was administered as a supplement to the monthly Labour Force Survey (LFS), it is possible to obtain the contemporaneously reported LFS records on labour-force state for each of the months that the person is in the LFS sample. These linked data are hence the same as the source of Canadian evidence on gross flows of labour, and brief comment on the nature of these data is in order at this point.[2]

Gross-flow data derive from the LFS, a monthly survey of about 53,000 dwellings representative of the civilian, non-institutionalized population aged 15 and over in the 10 provinces; data are available from the start of 1976, prior to which the LFS had a different format.[3] A respondent is surveyed for six consecutive months and, in each, is asked his or her current labour-force status, with the three categories being employed, unemployed, or not in the labour force (NLF). Matched record data are then derived by linking the same individuals in adjacent surveys, with approximately one-sixth of LFS respondents being new in any month, so that the base sample is about five-sixths that of the monthly LFS.

Two principal difficulties affect work with matched records from the LFS – missing data and classification errors.[4] Observations can be missed for many reasons, some of which may be correlated with labour-market activity; a censored LFS record of less than six months can often arise when the respondent has moved, for example, which may be related to change in employment status. Such non-random missing responses and attrition constitute a problem for almost all research that exploits panel data. In addition, matched record data are subject to potential classification error, whereby even random and uncorrelated errors in labour-force-state classification in one month induce upward bias in measured gross flows. In a simple example, one misclassification of status can lead to two spurious transitions, though the effect on the stocks of multiple misclassifications can be partially cancelling.

In the context of the LMAS and LFS linkage, both of these potential infirmities in the data are important, though the extent to which they vitiate conclusions based on these spell data remains unclear (for related discussion, see Blanchard and Diamond 1990 and Burda and Wyplosz 1990). A natural expectation would be that such classification-error problems could generate too many short (one-month) spells, analogous to the overstatement of gross flows found in that literature, though it is unlikely that this poses a major problem for spells of two or more months. There are no published reinterview data that would facilitate the types of corrections that have been performed in the United States.

For the LMAS-LFS match, data have been obtained from Statistics Canada for all persons in the longitudinal file of the 1986–87 LMAS. These LFS data are hence monthly, unlike the weekly data in the LMAS, and they cover a maximum of six months, not the two-year retrospective period covered by the LMAS. Furthermore, the LFS information categorizes agents into three states – employed, unemployed, and not in the labour force – rather than the four states attempted in the LMAS.[5] Finally, the LFS data themselves contain little demographic and related information. However, this situation can be remedied in the present case by matching the LFS data on an individual level to the demographic and other information from the LMAS. I refer to this matched dataset as the LMAS-LFS data.

The second avenue for empirical research in light of the LMAS filter is to adopt a simpler, two-state model of the labour market, coding all weeks as either employed or non-employed.[6] The portmanteau non-employment state encompasses unemployed, the LMAS "marginal" state (of wanting work but not searching for it), and non-participants. Since the LMAS correctly dates jobs, their complement is also correctly recorded.[7] Hence, provided that the analyst is prepared to group all non-employment spells together, the LMAS can be used to analyse such durations.

There are two principal drawbacks with this approach if the object of interest is unemployment, rather than non-employment. First, many of the non-employed are full-year non-participants, so that the longest durations correspond largely to people who have little real link to the labour market and who are poorly grouped with the unemployed, at least if defined on LFS terms. This problem can be rectified somewhat by omission of all left-censored non-employment spells – that is, spells that were already in progress at the commencement of the LMAS's two-year window. Focusing on fresh spells excludes full-year non-participants from the sample of interest.

Second, other groups move into and out of non-employment within a year (or within the LMAS's two years) and generate fresh spells of non-employment that do not correspond to unemployment as usually defined. The main problem of this type comes from movement into and out of education, which the LFS would code as out of the labour force rather than unemployment, but which, in a two-state model, will be confounded with unemployment spells under the non-employment grouping. Adjusting the sample to omit those below a certain age would be one expedient way of trying to reduce the extent of this difficulty. I also try using the self-reported reasons for first leaving employment in the two-year period covered by the LMAS, dropping respondents who reported leaving employment (and hence starting the fresh non-employment spell) because of retirement, ill health, other personal reasons, and education. While this adjustment cannot correctly rule out non-employment spells that may have started as unemployment and later turned into education, for example, and while it might also lead to the erroneous exclusion of a spell that began as ill health but became one of LFS-defined unemployment, it does represent a possible improvement over the straightforward use of all non-employment spells. I study both possibilities in the empirical work below.

LMAS-LFS RESULTS FOR UNEMPLOYMENT DURATION

I first address the microeconomic results obtained from using the LMAS-LFS dataset. My framework is a hazard model of the determinants of unemployment duration, so that the object of study is the probability of a spell ending in a given period, conditional on the spell being ongoing at the start of this period. This approach has three principal advantages over, say, regression-based estimates of the determinants of duration. First, it permits allowance for incomplete, right-censored spells that are still in progress at the end of the observation period (e.g. the LFS's six months). Second, it potentially permits determinants of duration to vary over time: when overall economic conditions within a particular region worsen during the course of a (lengthy) spell, the probability of a transit out of unemployment can be allowed to decline, for example. Of course, in relatively short spells, such time-varying covariates may not move enough to play a large role. Third, use of a hazard framework permits the probability of leaving unemployment to vary as the spell continues, displaying state or duration dependence of the sort that, at least in principle, could be a microeconomic foundation for hysteresis in the aggregate.[8]

In the present case, analysis begins with a particular version of the hazard framework – the proportional-hazards model (Cox 1972). This model allows the baseline hazard, $b(t, 0)$, which gives the escape probability at time t when all regressors are set to zero, to assume any shape. The effect of explanatory variables is then restricted to being proportional on this baseline, yielding an overall hazard $h(t,X)$ given by

$$h(t,X) = b(t,0)e^{X'\beta}, \tag{6.1}$$

where X is a vector of independent variables and β is a coefficient vector. Much recent work suggests that this model is useful to

Table 6.1
First-spell distribution in the LMAS-LFS data

No. of months	Right-censored	Complete	Total
1	1,109	2,751	3,860
2	606	825	1,431
3	414	341	755
4	395	106	501
5	294	0	294
Total	2,818	4,023	6,841

investigate, in addition to various parametric specifications that restrict the effect of duration on the hazard to following some assumed distribution (e.g. Weibull, logistic, Normal); see, for example, Ridder (1986). Moreover, for estimating the nature of any state dependence that might be present, the semi-parametric estimation of the baseline seems appropriate.

This model has been estimated using the LMAS-LFS data on monthly labour-force states. I consider all (fresh) unemployment spells that begin at any time in the LFS observation phase; such spells may either end in the window, in which case they are complete, or they may be still continuing when the subject is dropped from the LFS sample, in which case they are right-censored. I also restrict attention to the first such spell in the LMAS-LFS data for each person: there are 6,841 such spells, ranging from 1 to 5 months in length, and this distribution is tabulated in Table 6.1. I do not attempt an analysis of repeat spells with these short–time-frame data.[9]

Estimates of two specifications are presented in Table 6.2. In both, regional effects should be interpreted relative to a base (excluded) case of Ontario. Also, I have included a dummy variable indicating the month in which a particular unemployment spell started; these variables range from October 1986 to June 1987, the largest numbers being in January and February 1987 because of the design of the LMAS sample. However, this dummy variable has no effect on the other results, so it is omitted in all the model specifications reported in this subsection. I also investigated inclusion of variables indicating of unemployment insurance (UI) benefits receipt at some point during the year; this had little effect on the other coefficient estimates, though the UI effects themselves tended to be very imprecisely estimated. In the first set of results in Table 6.2, only the dummy variables for the Prairies are significant,

Table 6.2
Proportional-hazards estimates of determinants of unemployment duration

Determinants	*Equation 1*	*Equation 2*
Maritimes	–0.05	–0.06
	(0.05)	(0.05)
Quebec	0.00	0.02
	(0.06)	(0.06)
Prairies	–0.12*	–0.11*
	(0.05)	(0.05)
BC	–0.02	–0.01
	(0.06)	(0.06)
Male	–	–0.09**
		(0.03)
Married	–	0.00
		(0.04)
Visible minority	–	–0.10
		(0.09)
Age	–	–0.00
		(0.00)
Years of education	–	–0.00
		(0.01)
Number of children	–	0.04**
		(0.01)
Sample size	6,841	6,841
Log likelihood	–34,101	–34,089
p-value for χ^2 of exclusion of all independent variables	0.0528	0.0002

* and ** denote coefficients that are statistically different from zero at the 5 per cent and 1 per cent levels, respectively. Standard errors in parentheses.

lowering the hazard relative to Ontario. In the second equation, which adds to the regional variables a set of demographic characteristics from the LMAS, the male dummy variable acts to reduce the estimated hazard, while having a larger number of children tends to raise the hazard, with the significant negative effect for the Prairies still present.

Given these proportional-hazard models, the generated baseline hazards are graphed in Figures 6.1 and 6.2, respectively. While there are differences in these graphs according to the model estimated, they display striking similarity, with the baseline hazard out of unemployment falling from over 0.4 at one month to below 0.2 once a spell has reached four months. By construction, any five-month spell in the LMAS-LFS data must be right-censored (see Table 6.1),

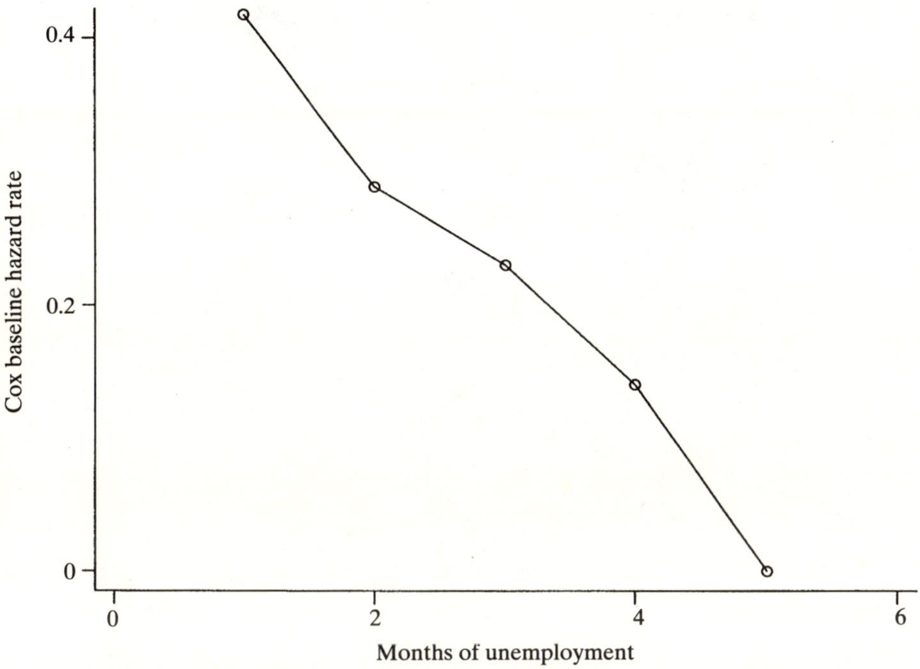

Figure 6.1
LMAS-LFS data, model 1

with no exits after five months ever being observed in the data. None the less, these graphs do suggest an interesting degree of duration dependence, controlling for the other determinants of unemployment duration, with longer spells leading to a decline in the hazard.

Two qualifications must be made to these results. First, no satisfactory allowance for the role of UI and other benefits can be made in these LMAS-LFS data, since the only information available from the 1986–87 LMAS is whether or not a subject ever received such a benefit at some point during a particular calendar year. This precludes any useful consideration of the timing of such benefits and the potential, found in the earlier Canadian work surveyed in chapter 4 above, for the hazard to change significantly around the weeks when a benefit is exhausted. Second, while the baseline hazards decline for each model presented, there may of course be non-random selection of individuals into these longer spells; this is the key to the state dependence *versus* heterogeneity debate in the

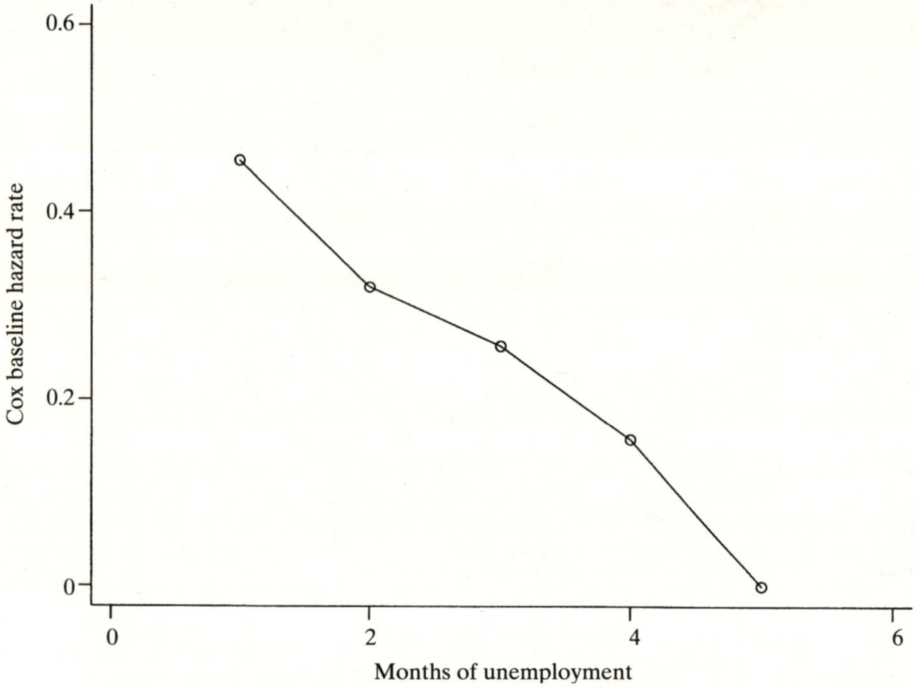

Figure 6.2
LMAS-LFS data, model 2

duration literature. Alternative specifications and alternative sets of variables to account for observed heterogeneity can shed light on whether this state dependence is robust.

To address robustness, I next look at four alternative parametric specifications – exponential, Weibull, logistic, and Normal – of the hazard out of unemployment. The exponential model imposes a constant hazard, so that

$$h(t) = \lambda, \tag{6.2}$$

and is accordingly the unique, memoryless distribution. On this view, no matter how long a spell has lasted, the conditional probability that it will end in the next short period Δt is the same, $\lambda\Delta t$. The Weibull model, in contrast, permits positive or negative duration dependence, with hazard

$$h(t) = \lambda p(\lambda t)^{p-1}, \tag{6.3}$$

nesting the exponential as a special case when $p = 1$. The logistic has hazard given by

$$h(t) = \frac{\lambda p\,(\lambda t)^{p-1}}{1 + (\lambda t)^{p}}, \tag{6.4}$$

while the Normal is simply

$$h(t) = \phi/\Phi. \tag{6.5}$$

The last two distributions both permit non-monotonic behaviour of the hazard for some ranges of parameter values.

Table 6.3 reports the results of estimating these four parametric models using the same set of explanatory variables as in the second specification of the proportional-hazards model. Perhaps not surprising, in view of the literature on misspecification resulting from imposition of inappropriate functional forms, these estimates differ, depending on the parametric form, and there is considerable variation in the implied nature of the hazard function. When a constant hazard is imposed, in the exponential case, the regional effect remains for the Prairies, as in the proportional-hazards estimates in Table 6.2, and it persists to some degree for the other three functional forms. Most other parameter estimates are fairly close to the results in Table 6.2. In the Weibull case, the key parameter is p in equation (6.3) above, and the point estimate of 1.51 implies a sharply rising hazard with increasing duration.[10] The confidence interval is quite tight for this parameter, implying decisive rejection of constancy of the hazard. In the logistic case, for which a value of p less than one would imply a hazard that declined monotonically with duration, the estimated value of 2.30 means that the hazard exhibits non-monotonic behaviour, rising and then falling. Lastly, in the normal case, this latter pattern is repeated, with the implied hazard at first rising and then falling with duration.

Overall, there is no uniformity to these various results from the alternative models of unemployment duration. The models that display declining hazard may be a consequence of true duration dependence or may, in part, be a reflection of inadequate controls and unobserved heterogeneity. Conversely, the parametric models that exhibit increasing hazard may also be true state dependence

Table 6.3
Alternative parametric models of the determinants of unemployment duration

Determinants	*Exponential*	*Weibull*	*Logistic*	*Normal*
Maritimes	–0.07	–0.06*	–0.04	–0.04
	(0.05)	(0.03)	(0.03)	(0.03)
Quebec	0.03	0.02	0.02	0.02
	(0.06)	(0.03)	(0.03)	(0.03)
Prairies	–0.11*	–0.08*	–0.07*	–0.06
	(0.06)	(0.03)	(0.03)	(0.03)
BC	0.00	0.01	0.03	0.02
	(0.07)	(0.04)	(0.04)	(0.04)
Male	–0.11**	–0.09**	–0.09**	–0.08**
	(0.03)	(0.02)	(0.02)	(0.02)
Married	0.00	–0.00	–0.00	–0.00
	(0.04)	(0.02)	(0.02)	(0.02)
Visible minority	–0.15	–0.14**	–0.09	–0.09
	(0.09)	(0.05)	(0.05)	(0.05)
Age	–0.00**	–0.00**	–0.00**	–0.00**
	(0.00)	(0.00)	(0.00)	(0.00)
Years of education	–0.00	–0.00	–0.00	–0.00
	(0.01)	(0.01)	(0.01)	(0.01)
Number of children	0.04**	0.04**	0.03**	0.03**
	(0.01)	(0.01)	(0.01)	(0.01)
Constant	–0.93**	–0.86**	–0.50**	–0.57**
	(0.13)	(0.07)	(0.07)	(0.07)
p estimate (at means)	1.00	1.51*	2.30	1.41
		(0.03)	(0.05)	(0.03)
Sample size	6,841	6,841	6,841	6,841
Log likelihood	–7,452	–6,983	–6,407	–6,242
Implied shape of hazard with respect to duration	Constant (imposed)	Rising	Rising, then falling	Rising, then falling

* and ** denote coefficients that are statistically different from zero at the 5 per cent and 1 per cent levels, respectively. Standard errors in parentheses.

(of the opposite sign); alternatively, they may result from an inappropriate parametric assumption being imposed on the data.[11]

In conclusion, there are two problems with the LMAS-LFS data used. First, the spells involved are necessarily relatively short, while evidence from other countries suggests that it is largely in longer spells of unemployment that genuine duration dependence may be found. Subject to some qualifications, this problem can be partially overcome by using the two-state definition of non-employment – our next subject. Second, a major non-stationarity in the economic environment, from the perspective of an unemployed person, is

Table 6.4
Distribution of first non-employment spells in the 1986–87 LMAS

No. of months	*Right-censored*	*Complete*	*Total*
1	494	4,156	4,650
2	305	2,183	2,488
3	292	1,543	1,835
4	686	1,494	2,180
5	297	877	1,174
6	233	737	970
7	393	830	1,223
8	144	675	819
9	173	655	828
10	216	827	1,043
11	144	417	561
12	367	310	677
13	199	173	372
14	113	140	253
15	212	98	310
16	342	80	422
17	272	46	318
18	167	33	200
19	238	21	259
20	103	7	110
21	164	7	171
22	52	6	58
23	82	1	83
24	76	1	77
Total	5,764	15,317	21,081

that associated with the potential exhaustion of UI benefits. Previous work with administrative records has of course found these effects to be large and important, as noted in chapter 4. However, in the LMAS for 1986–87 (and hence in the corresponding LMAS-LFS data), the only benefit information is whether or not an individual received benefits at any time during a particular calendar year, with no further timing information. As a consequence, the above results cannot correctly control for the timing of benefit exhaustion effects. This serious qualification must be borne in mind for the non-employment results that follow.

A TWO-STATE MODEL

I now examine results using data from the full LMAS dataset for 1986–87, with all weeks categorized as employment or non-employment.

Table 6.5
Proportional-hazards estimates of determinants of non-employment duration

Determinants	*Equation 1*	*Equation 2*
Maritimes	–0.19**	–0.22**
	(0.02)	(0.02)
Quebec	–0.18**	–0.22**
	(0.03)	(0.03)
Prairies	–0.13**	–0.14**
	(0.02)	(0.02)
BC	–0.08*	–0.07*
	(0.03)	(0.03)
Male	–	0.28**
		(0.02)
Married	–	0.22**
		(0.02)
Visible minority	–	–0.25**
		(0.05)
Age	–	–0.02**
		(0.05)
Years of education	–	–0.03**
		(0.00)
Number of children	–	0.00
		(0.01)
Sample size	21,081	21,081
Log likelihood	–141,641	–141,246
p-value for χ^2 of exclusion of all independent variables	0.0000	0.0000

* and ** denote coefficients that are statistically different from zero at the 5 percent and 1 percent levels, respectively. Standard errors in parentheses.

As noted above, such data are retrospective, with data collection being early in a calendar year (1987 or 1988) about the whole of the preceding calendar year (1986 or 1987). I again use only fresh spells that start within the observation period (which is now the full two years covered by the LMAS), though such spells may be completed or ongoing (i.e. right-censored) by the end of 1987. Finally, the focus remains on first spells for each individual, with no analysis of repeats.[12]

For the first spells to be modelled here, Table 6.4 gives the breakdown of spells by duration and completion status, grouped by month for comparability with the LMAS-LFS analysis above. However, since weekly data are actually available in this case, the duration analysis is performed at this finer level of disaggregation.

Figure 6.3
LMAS, model 1, full sample

Proportional-hazards estimates of the determinants of non-employment durations are given in Table 6.5, with Ontario again being the omitted region. In the equation where only regional controls are included, all four regions exert a negative influence on the hazard, relative to the Ontario base case, and all these estimated coefficients are significant. When demographic variables are added in the second equation, almost all the effects are again significant. The dummy variables for male or married exert a sizeable positive effect, while an additional year of education also raises the hazard, though to a lesser degree. Older workers and members of visible minorities, however, have a lower hazard, controlling for these other factors. Finally, in comparison with the analogous results for unemployment duration given in Table 6.2 above, the one difference that merits comment is the present significantly positive coefficient on the male dummy variable compared with the significantly negative coefficient on this variable in Table 6.2. I suspect that this difference stems from the somewhat greater preponderance of women in these

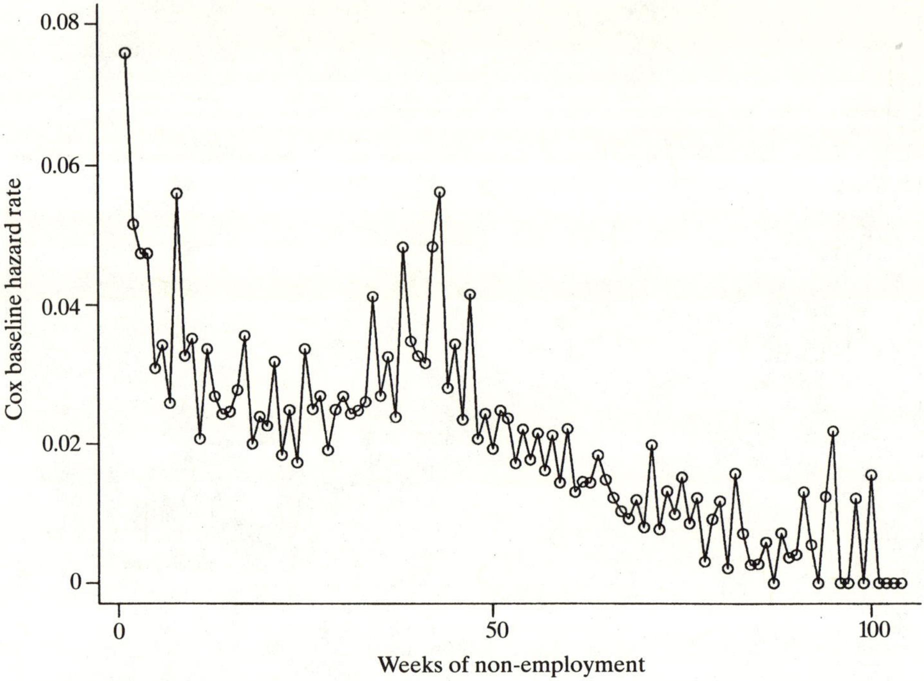

Figure 6.4
LMAS, model 2, full sample

non-employment spells – with these women not participating at some time during the LMAS's two years – so that a man experiencing such a spell has a higher probability of transition into employment.

Corresponding to these two sets of estimates, Figures 6.3 and 6.4 graph the baseline hazards, giving the estimated escape probability out of non-employment into employment when all the regressors are set to zero; there is one distinct value of this hazard for each of the durations up to 104 weeks. Across both cases, the pattern is very similar, and, broadly speaking, it resembles the declining hazard found earlier for unemployment duration in the LMAS-LFS data. In the present case, the decline is less sharp overall, and the hazard seems to be composed of three distinct segments. First, there is a rapid decline in the baseline hazard in the first month or so. Second, after the first month, the hazard is approximately flat – though noisy – out to durations a little short of one year. Third,

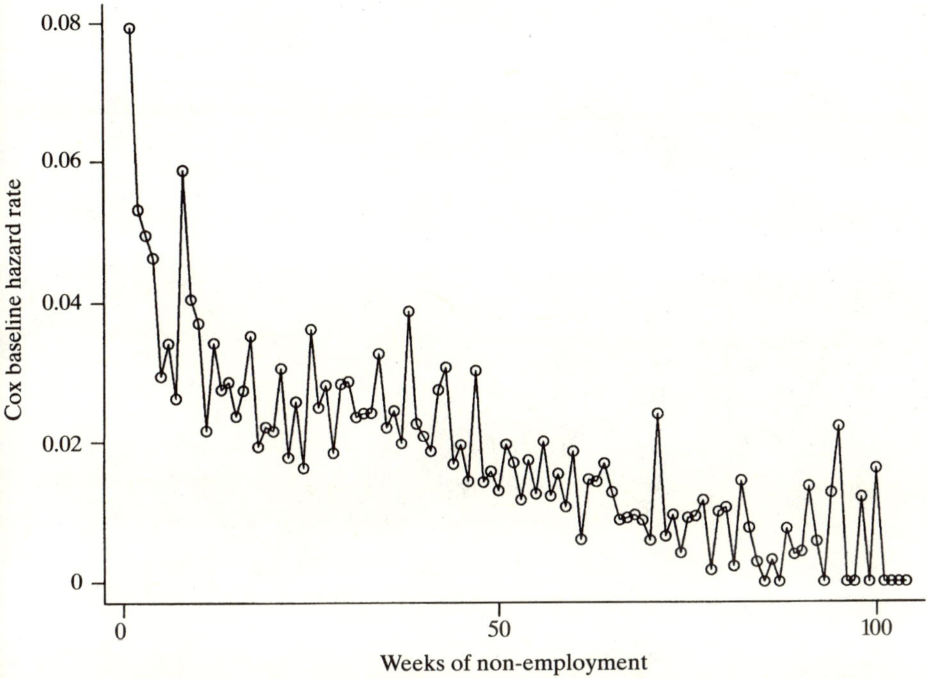

Figure 6.5
LMAS, model 1, non-young sample

beyond that, occurs a further decline, with a very low baseline hazard for the longest spells.

Finally, with regard to the proportional-hazard estimates, I have also re-estimated these models on two sets of subsamples. First, I have excluded all people under 25 years of age, in an effort to address the potential contamination of non-employment spells by periods of education. The parameter estimates for the remaining sample of 13,555 turn out, perhaps surprisingly, to be very close to those reported in Table 6.5 and are hence not reported here, though the associated baseline hazards are graphed in Figures 6.5 and 6.6. As with the full sample that includes the young, the pattern is one of decline, though with less clear flattening of the hazard between one and twelve months than in Figures 6.3 and 6.4. Second, I have further excluded, in addition to the young, any person whose first spell of non-employment is listed as starting for reasons of ill health,

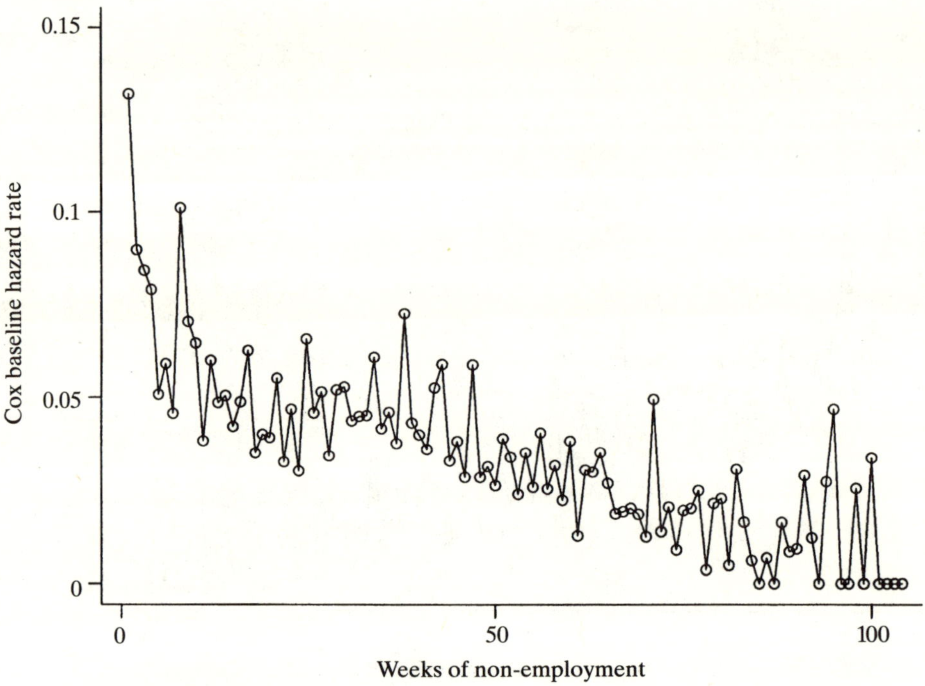

Figure 6.6
LMAS, model 2, non-young sample

education, or retirement. The problem of confounding unemployment and genuinely out-of-the-labour-force behaviour may thereby be avoided. This process yields a subsample of 12,822 observations, using only first spells only as before, and results analogous to those for the full sample are given in Table 6.6.

As can be seen, there are few major differences in the parameters when non-employment duration is estimated on this subsample. In addition, Figures 6.7 and 6.8 graph the associated baseline-hazard functions for the two equations estimated on this subsample. Again, the pattern is one of decline, steep in the first few weeks, then very gradual thereafter.

In addition, I have estimated the various parametric models using the LMAS's non-employment data (Table 6.7). In comparison with the second proportional-hazards equation reported in Table 6.5, most of the point estimates and confidence intervals display little change across the four parametric specifications. The significantly

Table 6.6
Proportional-hazards estimates of determinants of non-employment duration: subsample results

Determinants	*Equation 1*	*Equation 2*
Maritimes	–0.08*	–0.20**
	(0.03)	(0.03)
Quebec	–0.16**	–0.25**
	(0.04)	(0.04)
Prairies	–0.14**	–0.17**
	(0.03)	(0.03)
BC	–0.00	–0.03
	(0.04)	(0.04)
Male	–	0.39**
		(0.02)
Married	–	0.06*
		(0.03)
Visible minority	–	–0.24**
		(0.06)
Age	–	–0.02**
		(0.00)
Years of education	–	0.02**
		(0.01)
Number of children	–	0.05**
		(0.01)
Sample size	12,822	12,822
Log likelihood	–77,948	–77,464
p-value for χ^2 of exclusion of all independent variables	0.0000	0.0000

* and ** denote coefficients that are statistically different from zero at the 5 percent and 1 percent levels, respectively. Standard errors in parentheses.

positive male effect on the hazard persists in all four cases, which is notable given that this is the one respect in which these non-employment results differ from those for unemployment. The four models have differing implications for the hazard, however, with the imposed constancy of the exponential being supplanted by a monotonic decline in the more general Weibull case; this latter result differs from that in Table 6.3, of course. The logistic and the Normal both lead to a rising and then falling hazard, as before, though the peak now comes quite early.

Lastly, I have also done some experimentation with the Weibull model, making explicit allowance for gamma unobserved heterogeneity in the modelling of non-employment duration (a similar

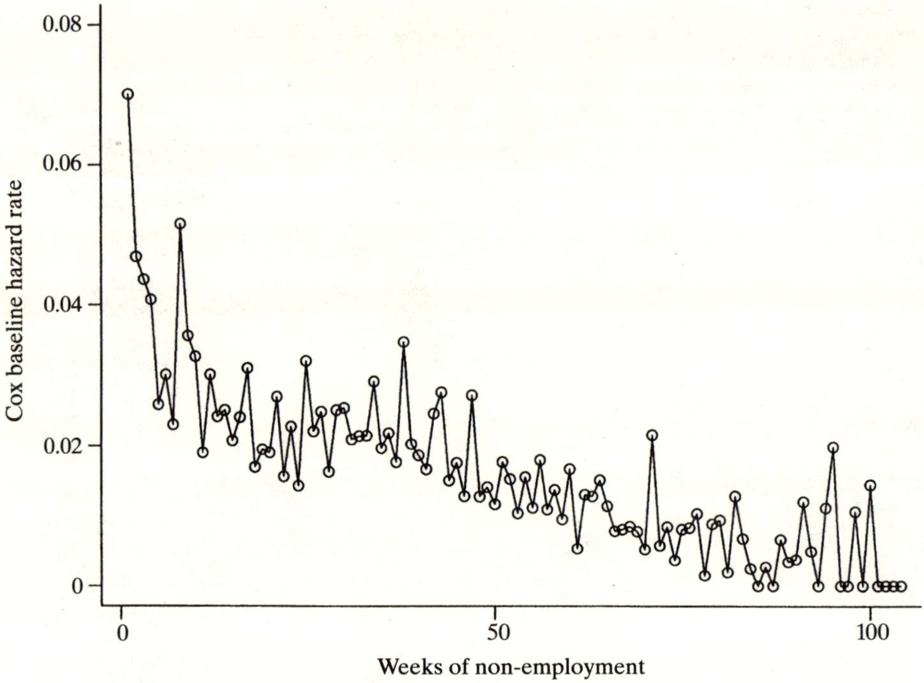

Figure 6.7
LMAS, model 1, restricted sample

model applied to LMAS-LFS unemployment duration failed to converge, however). In this approach, the survivor function is given by

$$S(t|\nu) = \nu \; e^{(-\lambda t)^{p}}, \tag{6.6}$$

where ν is the unobserved heterogeneity component that obeys a gamma distribution so that its density is

$$f(\nu) = [k^{R}/\Gamma(R)] \; c^{-k\nu} \; \nu^{R-1} \tag{6.7}$$

and the hazard is just

$$h(t) = \lambda \; p(\lambda t)^{p-1} \; [1 + ((\lambda t)^{p})/k]^{-k}. \tag{6.8}$$

The results of this model with an explicit specification for unobserved heterogeneity lead to a hazard function that declines with

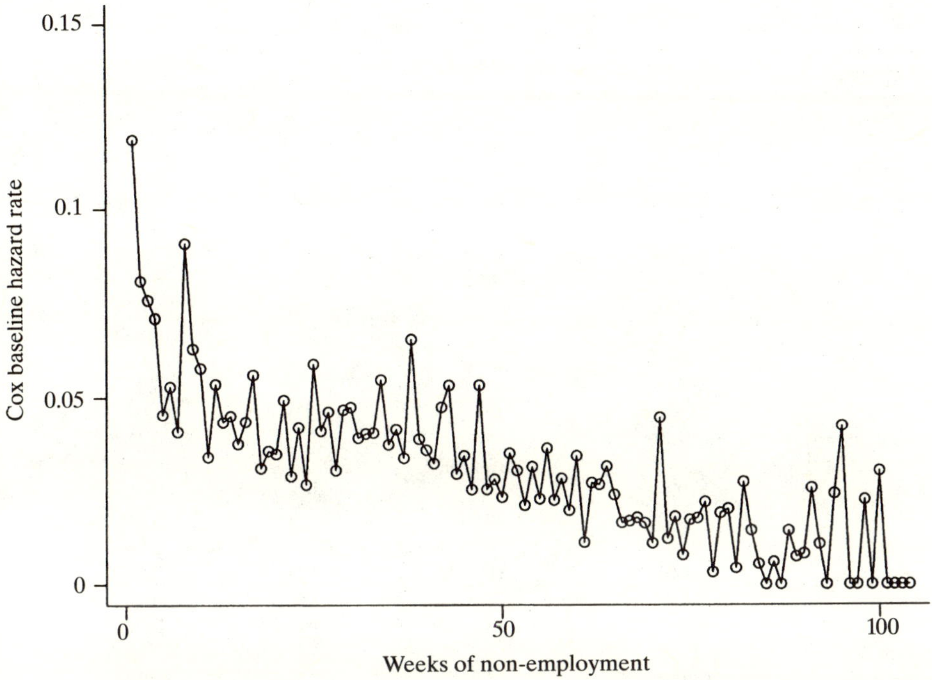

Figure 6.8
LMAS, model 2, restricted sample

duration, as in Table 6.7. The estimated value of $1/k$ is 0.43 (s.e. 0.04).[13] This figure suggests that, at least under the supposition that the Weibull is appropriate, the declining hazard reported in Table 6.7 is not simply an artifact of sorting caused by unobserved heterogeneity.

MULTIPLICITY AND MICROFOUNDATIONS OF MATCHING ANALYSIS

One final issue relevant to the multiple-equilibrium version of hysteresis, for which empirical evidence can be brought to bear, is the nature of the labour market's matching function. We saw in chapter 2 above that in the leading model of "thin markets" and trade-coordination equilibrium, one condition that can imply the existence of more than one equilibrium is increasing returns in the matching function; this remains true even if the underlying

Table 6.7
Alternative parametric models of the determinants of non-employment duration

Determinants	*Exponential*	*Weibull*	*Logistic*	*Normal*
Maritimes	–0.25**	–0.27*	–0.41**	–0.38**
	(0.02)	(0.03)	(0.03)	(0.03)
Quebec	–0.25**	–0.27**	–0.33**	–0.32**
	(0.03)	(0.03)	(0.04)	(0.04)
Prairies	–0.16**	–0.18**	–0.18**	–0.16**
	(0.02)	(0.03)	(0.03)	(0.03)
BC	–0.08**	–0.01*	–0.08	–0.07
	(0.03)	(0.03)	(0.04)	(0.04)
Male	0.33**	0.35**	0.32**	0.30**
	(0.01)	(0.02)	(0.02)	(0.02)
Married	0.24**	0.26**	0.27**	0.24**
	(0.02)	(0.02)	(0.02)	(0.02)
Visible minority	–0.28**	–0.31**	–0.31**	–0.29**
	(0.04)	(0.05)	(0.06)	(0.06)
Age	–0.02**	–0.02**	–0.02**	–0.02**
	(0.01)	(0.01)	(0.01)	(0.01)
Years of education	0.04**	0.04**	0.04**	0.04**
	(0.00)	(0.00)	(0.01)	(0.01)
Number of children	–0.00	0.00	–0.00	–0.00
	(0.01)	(0.01)	(0.01)	(0.01)
Constant	–3.41**	–3.40**	–2.94**	–2.85**
	(0.05)	(0.06)	(0.08)	(0.08)
p estimate (at means)	1.00	0.85	1.13	0.67
		(0.01)	(0.01)	(0.00)
Sample size	21,081	21,081	21,081	21,081
Log likelihood	–32,992	–32,683	–32,681	–32,465
Implied shape of hazard with respect to duration	Constant (imposed)	Falling	Rising, then falling	Rising, then falling

* and ** denote coefficients that are statistically different from zero at the 5 percent and 1 percent levels, respectively. Standard errors in parentheses.

production technology has constant returns to scale. Here I investigate whether Canadian data support such increasing returns in matching.

The approach taken follows that of Blanchard and Diamond (1989; 1990a), who recently investigated the form of the matching function using US data, with findings of mostly constant returns in the single-equation specifications on which they settled. The volume of new matches is taken here as the total monthly inflow into employment, be it from unemployment or from non-participation. No adjustment has been made for employment-to-employment direct job switches, and recalls are treated as new matches rather than as continuations of an old match.

The period for which data are available is 1976:2–1991:10, and we adopt the convention that a flow is dated by its second month. This period includes three recessions: a two-quarter slow-down at the start of 1980, a major recession in 1981–82, and the most recent economic downturn, when quarterly real GDP first declined in 1990:Q2.[14] Furthermore, these data are strongly seasonal, especially for flows into and out of the NLF state and for the young, for whom the educational year obviously has a strong influence (Jones 1993).

The model to be estimated is a Cobb-Douglas technology of matching, where the "inputs" are the logarithms of vacancies and unemployment, with allowance for a constant term and a time trend. Output from this technology – the dependent variable in the estimation – is the logarithm of employment inflow. The "vacancy" data employed are from the (old) help-wanted index,[15] so that, with the availability of this series coupled with that for the data on gross flows, the available sample is March 1976 to December 1988.[16] In all these series, seasonality is very strong. At the same time, the appropriate timing of the data should be the shortest available, to avoid problems with time aggregation, so the seasonal problem of the monthly data has to be recognized. Here I employ seasonally unadjusted data in every case and potentially allow for seasonal factors by including seasonal dummy variables in the estimation itself.[17] The leading alternative, which involves use of a prior seasonal-adjustment procedure (such as Census X-11), has statistical properties that are to some degree unknown and from which a suspicion of bias in the matching function estimates must remain.

Table 6.8 gives several sets of results from this estimation procedure. The first panel gives the results with no special allowance for seasonality. The Ordinary Least Squares (OLS) results imply a sum of coefficients on the logarithms of vacancies and unemployment of 1.26, a point estimate of increasing returns, but one cannot reject a sum of 1.00, the constant-returns case, at a reasonable level of significance. Imposing constancy of returns in the next column somewhat lowers both estimated coefficients. Both these estimates, however, have very low Durbin-Watson statistics, indicative of serious autocorrelation of the residuals, and the AR1 (Hildreth-Lu) estimate in the next column corrects for first-order serial correlation of the errors. The point estimate for the sum of the two input

Table 6.8
Matching-function estimates

	OLS	*OLS CRS*	*AR1 HiLu*	*IV*
NO SEASONALS				
Log vacancies	0.376**	0.295**	0.442**	–0.094
	(0.087)	(0.034)	(0.084)	(0.150)
Log unemployment	0.882**	0.705**	0.779**	–0.127
	(0.178)	(0.034)	(0.194)	(0.285)
Trend	–0.003**	–0.002**	–0.003*	–0.002
	(0.001)	(0.000)	(0.001)	(0.001)
Constant	–1.428	0.103	–0.994	7.286**
	(1.507)	(0.089)	(1.495)	(2.497)
Durbin Watson	0.844	0.850	1.838	0.837
p-value for CRS test	0.311	imposed	0.370	0.005
N	147	147	145	141
SEASONALS INCLUDED				
Log vacancies	–0.099	0.289**	0.278**	–0.130
	(0.057)	(0.016)	(0.017)	(0.091)
Log unemployment	–0.165	0.711**	0.692**	–0.232
	(0.125)	(0.016)	(0.011)	(0.200)
Trend	0.002**	–0.002**	–0.002**	0.002**
	(0.001)	(0.000)	(0.000)	(0.001)
Constant	–	–	–	–
Durbin Watson	2.490	2.033	1.988	2.452
p-value for CRS test	0.000	imposed	0.000	0.000
N	136	136	135	130

* and ** denote coefficients that are statistically different from zero at the 5 percent and 1 percent levels, respectively. Standard errors in parentheses.

coefficients is now 1.22, but, again, one cannot reject a sum of 1.00, the constant-returns case. Finally, the last column tries to tackle potential simultaneity associated with the timing of matches, vacancies, and unemployment by instrumenting the independent variables by their own lagged values (using the variable lagged 1–4 times).[18] This leads to very poor estimates, however, and it is accordingly hard to interpret the results. Finally, the second panel of Table 6.8 reports analogous estimates where each equation includes a full set of monthly dummy variables but excludes a constant term. Curiously, this seems to produce very odd estimates, even in the simple OLS case, suggesting that this way of allowing for a deterministic seasonal component accounts for too much of the important variation in the dependent variable.

Overall, while there may be room for further work on these matching issues, possibly by looking at data broken down on a regional basis,[19] the conclusion from Table 6.8 is not that increasing returns in matching are an important feature of the Canadian data. This conclusion echoes Blanchard and Diamond's (1989; 1990a) findings for the United States and Pissarides's earlier (1986) result using data from the United Kingdom, suggesting that one precondition for multiplicity of equilibria may not be satisfied. It also therefore corresponds to the results of Dagsvik and Jovanovic (1991) and Carruth and Oswald (1988) discussed in chapter 3, both of which found evidence for uniqueness in respective frameworks that each allowed for the possibility of multiplicity.

CONCLUSION

The conclusions that follow from the microeconomic investigations in this chapter are undoubtedly more mixed than the unambiguous interpretation placed on the macroeconomic results in chapter 5. While the short, contemporaneously reported unemployment spells in the LMAS-LFS dataset did give some indication of negative duration dependence, especially for the semiparametric estimates, this finding was not always confirmed when a number of parametric models of duration were estimated. For the longer, retrospective spells of non-employment, the results were somewhat more consistent across alternative models and displayed little apparent sensitivity to inclusion or exclusion of the young or to exclusion of some non-employment spells that, it was suspected, might not truly be unemployment. In each case, the finding was one of some negative duration dependence, though typically with rapid decline of the hazard in the first few weeks of a non-employment spell and slow decline from about one year out to two years; in between, the pattern in the semiparametric model was largely flat. Both data sources, then, suggest negative duration dependence, though in both cases the present inability to control for timing of eligibility and exhaustion of UI benefits must remain a major qualification. Lastly, study of an empirical matching function failed to uncover clear evidence of the increasing returns in matching that would constitute one foundation for hysteretic models of labour markets with multiple equilibria.

7 Conclusion and Policy Implications

An overall assessment of the importance of hysteresis in Canadian labour markets must take into account the range of evidence discussed above, both that by other researchers surveyed in chapter 4 and the new findings of chapters 5 and 6. I begin by summarizing the main results of this work, first at a macroeconomic level, then with regard to the microeconomic evidence that has been marshalled. I go on to discuss the degree of consistency or inconsistency in these results and to propose a way of thinking about their reconciliation.

The main thrust of the macroeconomic evidence must be said to go against the hypothesis of full hysteresis. While the univariate results on the time-series properties of the unemployment rate are suggestive of some non-stationarity, common sense implies that these results alone cannot be taken too literally. In contrast, most previous work on the relationship between the inflation rate and the level and change of the rate of unemployment found a significant role for the level, which would not be present under hysteresis, even though some recent work suggests that measurement problems may tend misleadingly to push such a level effect toward insignificance. In a detailed analysis of the one exception to these results, it was found that specifications that showed hysteresis are quite sensitive to a number of econometric and modelling assumptions and that, as a consequence, such results could not be regarded as robust.

The microeconomic evidence is naturally more partial in scope, and this factor should be kept in mind in making an overall assessment. Most of the microeconomic results in this book have been derived from a particular sample, the Labour Market Activity Survey (LMAS) longitudinal file for 1986–87, supplemented by the contemporaneous Labour Force Survey (LFS) records available for these individuals. While this group is, by construction, representative of the population of the ten provinces at the time of the survey, results derived from these data clearly cannot address changes in the microeconomic functioning of labour markets over time, especially over decades. Future researchers will be able to exploit the long-panel data promised by Statistics Canada's Survey of Labour and Income Dynamics, currently at an early stage. Finally, inability to control appropriately for timing and duration effects of participation in unemployment insurance (UI) benefits must remain a qualification to the results.

With these caveats, the microeconomic results do suggest some duration dependence in unemployment or non-employment spells, though the results remain somewhat mixed. For the (short) unemployment spells available from the LMAS-LFS dataset constructed for this study, while the semiparametric model gives some indication of negative duration dependence, all the parametric models estimated that permit a non-constant hazard function imply a range with positive duration dependence; in some cases, this behaviour is monotonic, in others not.

For the longer non-employment spells from the LMAS itself, the proportional-hazards models again show sensible parameter estimates and a declining baseline hazard. However, especially when all ages are included in the sample, such hazards appear to decline very early in a non-employment spell and then remain close to constant out to a year or so. Beyond that, hazard declines further, reaching a very low, conditional-transition probability by the longest spells in these data, which are close to two years. In parametric duration analysis, these results are to some degree supported, though again the findings do vary with the functional form adopted. Finally, some estimates of a matching function for the Canadian economy in the period 1976–88 did not give strong evidence of increasing returns in the matching technology, suggesting that, if multiple equilibria are important at the level of the macroeconomy, they are probably not based on this type of microeconomic foundation.

It is instructive to consider the relationship between the macroeconomic and the microeconomic results. There are several points to consider. First, differences in the time period and other details of estimation and modelling mean that there need be no necessary correspondence between a significant effect of the change of the unemployment rate in an empirical Phillips curve based on annual data covering a span of decades and robust negative duration dependence in unemployment spells from the 1986–87 LMAS.

Second, the results of this study in fact seem to be somewhat consistent across the two approaches, with a mixed pattern of state dependence at the microeconomic level and some weak evidence of hysteresis, in some cases, at the macroeconomic. One potentially useful approach to this interrelationship may be to think of the types of microeconomic duration dependence and other effects that could be consistent with the long lags on changes in unemployment seemingly required to generate macroeconomic evidence of hysteresis.[1] Overall, though, neither set of results strongly supports hysteresis and negative duration dependence.

Third, and most fundamental, it remains unclear even on a theoretical level what correspondence one *ought* to find between these two sets of results. Individual effects can be offsetting, for example, so that duration dependence at the microeconomic level might translate into little in the aggregate. This position is illustrated most clearly by Blanchard and Diamond (1994) in the context of their "ranking" model of unemployment durations, though the point is a more general one. In their model, for example, firms' (slight) preference for hiring the applicant with the shortest unemployment duration generates a declining hazard out of unemployment and gives rise to wage behaviour that depends on the pattern of unemployment duration in the population. However, throughout this model, such ranking determines only which applicant is hired and has *no* effect on total numbers: that is, it produces microeconomic state dependence but no macroeconomic effect in steady state. The contrast between partial-equilibrium analysis and the general equilibrium required for economy-wide results is not a new point, of course. Albrecht and Axell (1984) provide another clear illustration in the context of search theory and the analysis of UI effects. But novel or not, the point remains important to remember.

POLICY IMPLICATIONS OF THE RESULTS

Since the leading conclusion of this book has been against the hypothesis of hysteresis, the radical rethinking of macroeconomic policy that such a hypothesis might imply – with a traditional non-accelerationist Phillips curve as the policy menu – is rendered moot.[2] Fortin (1991, 794–7) provides a useful discussion of the issues that would be raised by such hysteresis, in the context of a particular linear policy function with nominal income targeting.[3]

Even without such a finding, however, there are three points that follow as implications of the present results. First, I consider measurement of the sacrifice ratio – the amount of temporary unemployment required to bring about a permanent reduction of one percentage point in the rate of inflation.[4] Howitt (1990b, 105), in a notable contribution to the Canadian debate on policy, has argued based on the experience of the 1980s that the cost of reducing inflation was about 4.7 per cent of (current) GNP per percentage-point drop in the rate of inflation. Assuming, more tentatively, a permanent gain of 1.875 per cent per year to GNP from the increased efficiency produced by the lower inflation, and summing these future gains, appropriately discounted,[5] Howitt calculates that the gain from the lower inflation outweighs the cost by something like a factor of 27 times.

Two qualifications are important, however. Laidler (1990) and Fortin (1990) both argued that, in the presence of hysteresis, the temporary/permanent breakdown in Howitt's calculation is no longer valid. If the loss of 4.7 per cent of current GNP were permanent, not temporary, the discounted cost would amount to 313 per cent of GNP. As noted above, however, this hysteresis condition does not seem to hold. In addition, Cozier and Wilkinson (1991) qualified Howitt's analysis in a number of respects, using data from a longer time period, controlling for commodity price shocks, and working directly with a measure of the output gap, rather than through an assumed Okun's-law coefficient, finding an estimated sacrifice ratio of about 2, less than half Howitt's figure.

In light of this debate, the results from chapter 5 are salient. While the finding was that estimates of an empirical Phillips curve were relatively unambiguous with regard to hysteresis-type effects, small changes in the estimated model could still have important effects for the implied sacrifice ratio.[6] That is, there remains considerable uncertainty regarding the cost of disinflationary policy, in addition to the often-acknowledged uncertainties that plague measurement of the benefits of such a policy.[7]

Second, a further area of uncertainty concerns the response of inflationary expectations to a disinflationary policy change (that is, a policy change designed to lower the rate of inflation), something that is not well captured by the standard empirical Phillips-curve approach. Some preliminary work on this issue using a non-linear Phillips-curve specification is presented by Laxton, Rose, and Tetlow (1993a, 16–20), who employ survey data from professional forecasters to proxy expectations. They generate steady-state simulation results with a 50–50, backward-forward–looking model of expectations that yields a temporary output loss (their equivalent of a sacrifice ratio) of 1.9 and an equivalent output gain of 0.8, though these figures rise to 5.2 and 1.7, respectively, in their purely backward-looking case (and fall to 0.2 and 0.2 in the extreme case of fully forward-looking expectations). While they note that their intermediate results correspond quite closely with those of Cozier and Wilkinson (1991), who employed purely backward-looking expectations and a linear specification, their precise numbers are probably less important than the general method of investigation.

Third, and closely related, there are uncertainties associated with measurement of the natural rate of unemployment. As the survey of past work revealed, existing knowledge yields only a very wide confidence interval for the natural rate, one that reasonably encompasses the majority of recent actual unemployment rates, and policy should take this ignorance into account.[8] In particular, with potential asymmetry of the loss function from policy mistakes associated with the plausible range of values for the natural rate, policy calculations must evaluate distribution of outcomes, rather than using the point estimate of the natural rate as though it were known with certainty.

Fourth and finally, though the central finding against hysteresis undercuts the type of fundamental rethinking of the stance of macroeconomic policy-making that some have proposed, this does not imply generally inactivist policy. Evidence of negative duration dependence may suggest benefits to be had from a more activist UI program, for example, though such conclusions would ideally be buttressed by individual-level data with information on timing and duration of program participation. Also, as noted in the preceding subsection, partial-equilibrium effects estimated with existing programs may not carry over in a simple way to the new general equilibrium under an alternative policy regime. None the less, much in the microeconomic results is suggestive of the potential for beneficial microeconomic policy intervention, and further study in this area is clearly warranted as new and better longitudinal data become available.

Notes

CHAPTER ONE

1 For a valuable comparison of the labour-market effects of the recessions of 1981–82 and 1990–92, including use of a cumulative-impact measure of the overall depth and duration of a recession, see Picot, LeMaître, and Kuhn (1994). By this measure, though the recession of the 1990s was shallower than that of the early 1980s, its greater overall length led to a 28 per cent greater drop in cumulative labour volumc and to a 68 per cent greater increase in cumulated unemployment (p. 4.5). On the particular effect on the youth labour market, see Sunter (1994).

2 Friedman refers to the "Walrasian" system of general-equilibrium equations, named after Léon Walras, who developed the idea of general economic equilibrium.

3 An innovative theory of the natural rate based on an explicit treatment of turnover flows in the presence of imperfect information is Salop (1979). In his rich model, equilibrium at the natural rate can involve both voluntary and involuntary unemployment, the latter being structurally rooted in the frictions in the economy. Moreover, this equilibrium contains components of both search and disguised unemployment (see also Hall 1970).

4 Note that there are important questions about the consistency and comparability of these historical unemployment rates; it would be

unwise to compare 1982 and 1930 levels other than informally. For Canada, data for 1954–93 are drawn from Statistics Canada, *Historical Labour Force Statistics* (various issues); earlier figures are from the ILO, *Yearbook of Labour Statistics* (various issues). For the United States, data since 1930 are from US Department of Commerce, Economics and Statistics Administration, *Business Statistics* (various issues); earlier data are from the ILO, *Yearbook of Labour Statistics* (various issues). Data pertain to the civilian, non-institutionalized population in the following age ranges: for Canada, aged 14 and over for 1921–53 and aged 15 and over for 1954–93; for the United States, aged 14 and over for 1921–45 and aged 16 and over for 1946–93.

5 Though one of the prime formulators of the natural-rate hypothesis, Phelps was also one of the first to note the potential for hysteresis effects. See his 1971 discussion reprinted in Phelps (1979, 97–107).

6 General and somewhat abstract characterizations of hysteresis and discussion of its wider philosophical implications are provided by Franz (1990), Cross (1993b), and Katzner (1993).

7 Figure 1.1 above illustrates the emergence of the gap between Canada and US unemployment rates following the recession of 1981–82, a point to which I return below.

8 There may not, however, be a unique value for the sacrifice ratio in a number of plausible circumstances. Examples where the value would likely not be a constant include the cases of expectations responding to a policy change, of asymmetric reaction to positive and negative shocks, and of policy changes that might be introduced gradually or very rapidly.

9 The recent state of play in this policy debate is well summarized in two edited volumes (Lipsey 1990, York 1990). I return below to several of the contributions.

10 John Crow did recognize this potential implication of hysteresis when he was governor of the Bank of Canada; see Crow (1992, 6–7).

11 The reason the LMAS provides reliable information only on jobless spells, rather than on unemployment, stems from its questionnaire, which implies a tendency for unemployment spells that end in withdrawal from the labour force, rather than in employment, to be under-recorded. Jones and Riddell (1995) document this problem, which is discussed in detail in chapter 6 below.

12 Hazard models were first employed in the analysis of survival, such as survival of heart-transplant patients. Hence, the probability of an

"exit" (from life, in such a case) is termed a hazard, though in many contexts – such as the present study of transitions from unemployment to employment – the negative connotation of "hazard" does not apply.

CHAPTER TWO

1 Solow (1985) is another early reference on these types of models. The bibliography to Lindbeck and Snower (1988) contains reference to extensions beyond the simple framework sketched here.
2 See also the related analyses in Blanchard and Summers (1987a; 1987b). Blanchard and Summers (1988) emphasize the need for theories of "fragile" equilibrium, a situation where shocks can have a large impact and where outcomes may be history-dependent, and sketch some models with perverse demand or supply curves that can give rise to such properties.
3 Lindbeck and Snower (1988, chaps. 9 and 10) provide further analysis of these types of duration effects.
4 Another piece of pertinent evidence is given by Layard, Nickell, and Jackman (1991, 109–11). They present an approximate calculation based on plausible parameter values in a model with an aggregate wage equation driven by bargaining and conclude that such a framework gives a very small degree of unemployment persistence from insider power.
5 For further discussion of the role of insider-outsider models and the timing of wage-setting, relative to the timing of shocks, see Ball (1990).
6 The major alternative to this assumption of uniform layoff risk is a seniority-based model, as developed by Grossman (1983), for example. The work by Drazen and Gottfries (1987) discussed below does allow for such seniority-based layoffs.
7 Whether or not contracts do lie on the firm's demand curve for labour is the subject of a lively debate, both theoretically and empirically. See especially McDonald and Solow (1981), Brown and Ashenfelter (1986), MaCurdy and Pencavel (1986), and Espinoza and Rhee (1989) for the main points of discussion. For analysis of the relationship between the insider-outsider view and the dynamic properties of the labour-demand model, see Jones and McKenna (1989). For a model of the behaviour of a "dynamic" union, see Jones and McKenna (1994).

8 Such wages may occur with or without unions, of course, though it can be difficult to determine the true degree to which seniority drives wages (as opposed to some third factor, such as the quality of worker-job match, determining both seniority and wages). On this, see Abraham and Farber (1987), Altonji and Shakotko (1987), Brown (1989), and Topel (1991).

9 One interesting extension that they pursue is the observability or non-observability of old workers' marginal products.

10 The same result would follow from an increase in wage demands.

11 There is an extensive literature in international trade theory that explores such hysteretic effects driven by less-than-perfect competition. See, for example, Dixit (1989) and Grossman and Helpman (1990). For more on hysteresis and the theory of investment under uncertainty, see Dixit (1992) and the references therein.

12 An alternative formulation of the feedback from unemployment to worker's employability, drawing on the large social-psychology literature on the effects of unemployment, is based on the idea of "helplessness" induced by unemployment. Darity and Goldsmith (1993) discuss this literature and the extent to which it is distinct from or corroborated by the econometric literature on duration-dependence.

13 This work extends the simple models sketched by Hargreaves Heap (1980), an influential early paper on the implications of hysteresis.

14 It thereby neglects the role of unemployment per se.

15 Möller (1990) develops an explicit model with linear deterioration of human capital and shows that it implies a Gompertz-Makeham–type distribution for unemployment spells – an implication that is found to be not inconsistent with West German labour-market data for 1984–87.

16 On the supply side of the labour market, Vendrik (1993) proposes a novel theory based on habit formation with respect to consumption and labour supply, one implication of which is the potential for hysteresis (and in some cases path-dependence of the adjustment path to a unique equilibrium, a phenomenon Vendrik terms "quasi-hysteresis").

17 Relatedly, Price (1992) develops a model to formalize the effects of a deterioration of human capital and demonstrates two sets of suggestive results. First, there is a unique stationary equilibrium that involves unemployment when workers are infinite-lived (in addition to corner solutions at zero and "full" employment), though human-capital effects can operate to render the middle equilibrium unstable.

Second, in the finite-lived model, there may be multiple equilibria: though the (flow) supply locus slopes upward in (wage, employment) space, the (flow) demand locus has an ambiguous sign that may result in multiple supply-demand intersections.

18 See, for example, Adams (1988, 394).

19 Graafland and Huizinga (1990) show that employers' use of unemployed durations as a screening device will not necessarily lead to short-term shocks having long-term effects, however, and argue that something additional – such as wages that are tied to workers' ages – is required for this hysteretic result.

20 Related work is presented in Ball (1989).

21 King (1990) presents a stochastic model with coexisting frictional and long-term unemployment that exhibits a "local hysteresis effect," in that the overall unemployment rate at each Lucas-Prescott location (Lucas and Prescott 1974) depends on the recent history of technology shocks at that site. For some related Canadian evidence, see Samson (1988).

22 Such an aggregate effect does not have to follow, however; whether it does will depend on the interaction of job searchers who are recipients of unemployment insurance benefits and those who are not recipients.

23 In essence, this implies that government policies are being thought of as endogenous to the model.

24 This type of distinction is noted in Howitt (1990a), which studies a number of abstract coordination-failure models and analyses the effects of non-parametric learning processes on the equilibria reached.

25 As an example of the empirical issues that might be involved, Price (1992, 207–11) argues that the rapid decline in British unemployment at the end of the 1980s is more indicative of multiple equilibria than of a hysteresis model, which he characterizes as displaying high persistence and sluggish behaviour.

26 A related concept is Summers's (1988) notion of fragile equilibria, whereby small changes in exogenous variables produce large movements in the endogenous variables of interest, even if the underlying model displays uniqueness and stability, as conventionally defined.

27 In addition to these approaches, hysteresis and multiplicity of equilibria have been adopted as linchpins in some variants of "post-Keynesian economics." Some central references in these lively debates are Cross (1990a; 1990b; 1993a; 1993b), Davidson (1991;

1993), Arestis and Skott (1993), Issac (1993), Katzner (1993), and Setterfield (1993).

28 There may well be other mechanisms that an employer can use to induce workers not to shirk, and some economists have argued that such alternative means of eliciting effort, such as explicit or implicit bonding, vitiate the strong claims made of efficiency-wage theory. For an overview of the debate, see Carmichael (1990) and Lang and Kahn (1990).

29 See the papers in Benhabib (1992) for further discussion of non-linear dynamics and limit cycles.

30 A sceptical view of the relevance of solutions with multiplicity is given by B.T. McCallum (1989, 241–8).

31 For further references on the periodic and aperiodic properties of non-linear dynamic systems, see Day (1982; 1983) and Grandmont (1985).

32 An early statement of these ideas is Heller (1986).

33 The model presented in Durlauf (1993), for example, consists of: conditional probability measures that give individual actions conditional on events; a notion of equilibrium when these conditional probability measures are compatible, and hence of a joint-probability measure over all agents; and a notion of long-run equilibrium associated with an invariant probability measure (i.e. where the economy can settle down with no tendency to change). The concept of non-ergodicity is that a set of conditional probability measures can yield multiple invariant probability measures.

34 A recent work that explores a structuralist theory of how the "natural rate" of unemployment might be altered by a variety of shocks is Phelps (1994). Building on the general equilibrium formulation of the natural rate by Salop (1979), discussed above, Phelps's model formulates how real shocks push the natural rate up and down and addresses how the actual rate of unemployment follows this moving target. Relative to earlier work, the theory has the key property that the response of the natural rate to a technological advance is transitory (so that ongoing increases in productivity are consistent with a comparatively constant unemployment rate), and Phelps's model elaborates central roles for disturbances from real interest rates and transfer payments.

CHAPTER THREE

1 An example of this standard approach is Blanchard (1981), where the "hump-shaped" response of output to temporary shocks is detailed

and analysed along traditional, multiplier-accelerator lines, reinterpreted in light of rational-expectations developments in modelling.

2 Recently, Beaudry and Koop (1993) argued that previous results on the persistence of shocks may have been biased by an imposition of symmetry. When the impulse response of US GNP is allowed to be asymmetric, their findings are of strong and persistent positive shocks but of small and transitory effects from recessions.

3 Romer (1989), in a comment on Durlauf (1989), develops a simple framework for differentiating the persistence properties of supply and demand shocks, based on instrumenting demand movements, and finds that output changes driven by known shifts in aggregate demand are considerably more persistent than general changes in output. Though such results always depend on the choice (and validity) of the instruments, this result suggests that purely supply-based explanations of strong persistence may understate the role of demand-side effects.

4 He also examines evidence for a smaller number of countries for earlier years.

5 The longest period covered is for the United States; it runs from 1873 to 1986.

6 See also Alogoskoufis and Manning (1988b).

7 Their set of countries does not include Canada, however.

8 In this sense, their study perhaps overcorrects for earlier work that sought to attribute all changes in unemployment to changing structural determinants such as demographic factors.

9 Ball also investigates quarterly data that yield 65 episodes of disinflation in 19 moderate-inflation OECD countries.

10 Quarterly data based on disinflations of 1974:Q2–1976:Q4 and 1981:Q1–1986:Q4 give very similar estimates of the sacrifice ratio.

11 This suggests the broad validity of the credibility approach in Sargent (1983). For important related discussion that questions the importance of staggered contracts, given credibility, see Ball (1994).

12 Another area that should be noted briefly is the examination of measures of firing costs, as a direct attempt to proxy for the difficulty of replacing insiders (e.g. Lindbeck 1989, 513–15). Bertola (1990) provides evidence of essentially *no* relationship between measures of these turnover costs and the average level of unemployment in the 1970s and 1980s. There is, however, some apparent link between these costs and the degree of persistence in unemployment. See also the extension of his work in Ball (1990, 466–9).

13 Given the specification, we have $v = u + e/(1 - s)b$.

14 It appears that a moving average term is also needed.

15 Brunello (1990) examines, along similar lines, the Japanese evidence for hysteresis. The main finding, perhaps surprising, is that the Japanese economy seems to display as much hysteresis as many European economies, with Brunello's reading of the key difference between Japan and Europe being the degree of indexation to real shocks. Contrast, however, Coe (1988), whose evidence from aggregate wage equations for eight countries includes little evidence of hysteresis for Japan.

16 This approach solves the problem in Blanchard and Summers's (1986) original formulation – that expected future wages did not enter into labour demand, despite the adjustment-cost motivation.

17 An alternative empirical approach is directly to investigate evidence on union membership and employment, together with the links between these magnitudes and wage levels. Burda (1990) presents some results along these lines for union membership in the Federal Republic of Germany, finding evidence of membership hysteresis effects.

18 Some of the exogenous data may not be observable, however.

19 That is, it depends only on the current state (and not, for example, on how that particular state was reached).

20 Jones (1989) used detailed job-search data collected in a British survey in September 1982 to test for increasing returns in the search process and failed to discover any significant departure from constant returns.

21 This single-equation set of estimates, however, may have important simultaneity biases, and Blanchard and Diamond's instrumental-variables estimates are much more suggestive of increasing returns.

22 The two sectors are manufacturing and non-manufacturing in their empirical implementation.

23 This corresponds to an exponential distribution for unemployment spells, the only distribution with the "memoryless" property of no true duration dependence.

24 Graafland (1991) examines insider-outsider models of wage-setting and duration models of unemployment-vacancy dynamics for the Netherlands in the 1980s, finding little support for the former interpretation but clear evidence in favour of the latter. Additionally, see Lever (1991).

25 Related analyses of long-term unemployment include Flateau, Lewis, and Rushton (1991) for Australia and Neudorfer, Pichelmann, and Wagner (1990) for Austria.

26 In this discussion, long-term unemployment involves those unemployed for at least twelve months.

27 Miller (1988, 400–1), however, argues that the existence of a stable relationship between the number of long-term unemployed and total unemployment implies that the concept of a natural rate remains applicable.

28 Budd, Levine, and Smith (1988, 51–61), for instance, present interesting evidence on the effects of long-term unemployment in the wage equations of the macroeconomic model developed by Britain's London Business School.

CHAPTER FOUR

1 See also Kaliski (1987), Corak (1991a; 1991c; 1993b), and Osberg (1991).

2 This cyclical measure avoids the necessity of adjusting the overall rate of unemployment for demographic changes that might reasonably be thought of as affecting the natural rate itself.

3 They were unable to reject this accelerationist restriction at a 5 per cent confidence level.

4 Though there is only a temporary reduction in the flow rate of output (absent hysteresis), while the inflation reduction so generated is permanent, there has been an overall loss in the aggregate stock of output summed over all periods. I thank a referee for suggesting this clarification.

5 They use a measure of potential output from the Bank of Canada's RDXF model. See below for further discussion of this and other measures of the output gap.

6 One query about these results is whether Cozier and Wilkinson's model allows enough time for the tightness measure to operate, noting that their data is quarterly rather than annual. I return to this issue in some detail below.

7 For the labour-market variant of their model, the gap variable is defined as the difference between the actual rate of unemployment and the Bank of Canada's estimate of the natural rate.

8 The alternative would be to employ some sort of Okun's law to link unemployment and output.

9 Cozier and Wilkinson (1991, Table 4, p. 22) also examine four alternative measure of the output gap constructed using a linear trend, a quadratic trend, a Hodrick-Prescott moving average, and a series derived from the Bank's RDXF model. If we neglect the linear specification as

unreasonable, they find that estimated sacrifice ratios were usually a little higher for the quadratic model than for the gap measures based more directly on past values. Scarth (1993, 472–4) observes that these procedures implicitly assume no hysteresis when constructing the gap measure and further argues that these relative results suggest that Cozier and Wilkinson's estimates of the sacrifice ratio may be biased downward.

10 This latter result is suggestive of hysteresis, of course, though the authors state that they prefer the H-P filtered model's performance.

11 Only the United Kingdom also exhibits this property, while the United States, Japan, Germany, Australia, New Zealand, Italy, and France do not. The authors find some evidence of hysteresis in Italy and, recently, the United States.

12 It rises from 0.6 to 2.3 and from 0.8 to 1.3 in the period 1981:1–1993:1, using the fixed- and increasing-sample approaches, respectively (p. 12).

13 The reason for using the adult-male unemployment rate to measure labour-market tightness is presumably that it may have been less affected by structural changes over the sample period than, say, the overall unemployment rate. (See, for example, note 2 to this chapter.) However, no evidence is adduced in support of this proposition.

14 This was not the Bank's professed target throughout all of the period 1957–90 for which the model is estimated, however.

15 In fact, Blanchard and Summers were keen to avoid attribution of more than a small part of their insider-outsider modelling to the presence of unions, especially in Europe (and not in the United States), though most subsequent interpreters of their work have regarded the degree of unionization as key.

16 Fortin (1993) also contains some discussion of the cross-country relationship, if any, between inflation and the rate of productivity growth. This uses the growth model adapted to allow for human capital as developed by Mankiw, Romer, and Weil (1992) and follows on the work of Cozier and Selody (1992). Fortin's main result is that analysis of data for the OECD countries cannot reject the view that inflation has no effect on the permanent rate of productivity growth. There is, however, some evidence that a variety of specifications and alternative variables were tried before this result was reached (see Fortin 1993, 16 n 5).

17 The point estimate is calculated as the ratio of the change coefficient to the sum of the change and the level coefficients.

18 Relatedly, Fortin, Keil, and Symons's (1994) preliminary work using a panel of Canadian regions and demographic groups finds that lagged unemployment has a coefficient of about 0.65 when incorporated in a reduced-form specification with a dozen or so other explanatory variables, including some detailed UI-related regressors.

19 For a briefer account that is nuanced more favourably toward hysteresis, see Fortin (1994, 82–4).

20 This last trend amounts to a two-sided, moving-average filter.

21 This is roughly in the middle of prior estimates for Canada and the United States.

22 Positive output gaps might be too large and negative output gaps might be too small, given non-linearity.

23 Practically speaking, the non-linearity is conceptualized as either a kink, in which case output gaps have a larger effect if positive, or as a quadratic specification, in which case the square of the positive output-gap measure is employed (Laxton, Rose, and Tetlow 1993a, 4 and Tables 1 and 2, pp. 12–13). The results suggest that inflation moves up quickly in response to excess demand but is relatively slow to decline when the overall level of demand in the economy weakens.

24 The investigation of Lipsett and James (n.d.), discussed above, also failed (see p. 10) to find any significant non-linearities in the sample period as a whole.

25 In recent exploratory work that is also relevant to the measurement of a natural rate, Kuhn and Robb (1994) address the Canadian evidence for the hypothesis of Juhn, Murphy, and Topel (JMT) (1991), based on US data, that declining wage levels for the unskilled have led to voluntary reductions in labour supply and hence to a rise in unemployment (see also Murphy and Topel 1987). Using annual Canadian data for 1971–91, Kuhn and Robb exhibit some evidence consistent with JMT's theory, provided that the unskilled have high enough elasticities of labour supply. But they find two pieces of evidence that run counter to this reading – first, there was no corresponding decrease in unskilled-male unemployment in the years 1971–77, a period when there was substantial real wage growth for this group; and second, unemployment of Canadian women increased over the period 1971–91 as a whole, despite strong increases in wages at all skill levels.

26 This estimate covers the entire period subsequent to the 1971 UI reforms.

27 Another issue that should be kept in mind is the essentially arbitrary nature of the definition of unemployment. While there are important reasons, to do with historical and international consistency, to adhere to a standard definition of unemployment (which amounts to a job-search requirement in most cases), some persons counted as unemployed may exert little pressure on the labour market, and some not counted as unemployed may move into jobs quite quickly. For useful discussion of Canadian alternative measures of unemployment, see Devereaux (1992). For analysis of a unique Canadian set of microdata that permits a more formal econometric treatment of these measurement issues, see Jones and Riddell (1993).

28 For the period from September 1977 to November 1978, the regional extended benefits were based on unemployment rates in 16 regions. After November 1978, the number of benefit regions increased to 48; furthermore, there were some changes in the definitions of these regions in the early 1980s.

29 This calculation is not exactly the figure warranted by the 48 benefit regions used in the administration of the regional UI system, however. The main potential difficulty for the calculation that Milbourne, Purvis, and Scoones (1991) present is that intra-provincial variation in unemployment experiences might be economically significant, though missed by their figures.

30 Though clearly an artifact of their model, the behaviour of this group clearly parallels the stylized "10-40" characterization of work-unemployment experiences in the most depressed regions of Canada. See Corak (1992, 3.3 and 3.15), which presents evidence on the "10-40 syndrome" discussed by the Forget Commission.

31 Unemployment (measured by the monthly household-based Labour Force Survey) and the number of UI beneficiaries are *not* the same thing and, especially recently, exhibit a number of interesting differences. Lévesque (1987; 1989) provides an early discussion, and Barnes and Picard (1992) suggest that UI claims operated as a leading indicator of unemployment, anticipating turning points of unemployment by an average of ten months over the past two decades. However, Roy (1994) notes that this relationship seems to have weakened considerably in the early 1990s, reflecting the changing role of long-term unemployment (and UI benefit exhaustion) and the growing importance of students and the self-employed in the pool of unemployed. Also, Storer and Van Audenrode (1993)

attempt to model the Canadian UI take-up rate, based on evidence from the Canadian Survey of Displaced Workers, though their results naturally hinge on imputation of UI eligibility.

32 In related preliminary work, Fortin, Keil, and Symons (1994) report a back-of-the-envelope calculation based on their results using a Canadian panel of regions and demographic groups for the 1963–91 period. Using a figure of 0.006 for the sensitivity of reduced-form unemployment to a "wage subsidy" (as they view the regional, extended UI feedback mechanism), they conclude that the 1977 legislative changes to the UI system would have altered their autoregressive parameter for unemployment from 0.67 to 0.70 – a small effect that clearly cannot compare to the actual change in unemployment.

33 In addition to these studies that address aspects of Milbourne, Purvis, and Scoones's thesis and related concepts, there has recently been considerable research on the effects of the Canadian UI program. Notable contributions include Green and Riddell (1993a; 1993b), on disentitlement effects and the role of variable entrance requirements; Osberg, Erksoy, and Phipps (1993), on distributional effects of UI; Corak (1994a), on temporary layoffs and recalls; and Ferrall (1994), who develops an explicitly structural model to study UI and the youth labour market (in both Canada and the United States). Some of this work is covered in Corak's (1994b) useful survey.

34 Notice, though, the issues raised in note of this chapter regarding the growing discrepancies between UI claimants and unemployment itself.

35 Jones (1993) presents the basic evidence on the properties of Canadian gross flows since 1976, based on the Labour Force Survey.

36 For example, a "MATCH" variable is defined as the ratio of the proportion of the unemployed with a high-school diploma or less to the proportion of the employed with similar low qualifications (Gross, n.d., 36).

37 The reason is the "LMAS filter" of non-employment states detailed in Jones and Riddell (1995). In brief, the problem with the LMAS data on unemployment duration is that, as a consequence of the nature of the LMAS questionnaire, the only unemployment spells that are recorded are those that end in a job and those that are ongoing at the end of December in the year in question. Thus unemployment spells that end in withdrawal from the labour force (because of discouragement, family reasons, or a decision to undertake education, for example) are typically missed, and the durations

available from the LMAS are hence a filtered version of the true durations in the Canadian economy.

38 These are based on LFS gross-flow data so that the potential problems of classification error associated with such linked-record data should be borne in mind. See, for example, Abowd and Zellner (1985).

39 This was the example of exponentially distributed durations presented in chapter 3, above.

40 Ham and Rea find some sign of lagged duration dependence, whereby the length of a previous spell of unemployment has a significant effect on the hazard out of unemployment in the current spell; see column 6 of their Table 3 (340). This result is maintained even with the addition of the industry's unemployment rate at the start of the preceding spell (this attempting to control for a non-stationary economic environment that could produce spurious lagged dependence).

41 Two other studies that deal with these issues, both using small samples drawn from southeast Montreal, are Ducharme, Felteau, and Roy (1992) and Fortin and Prévost (1993). The latter study discusses some implications of its findings for hysteresis at the macroeconomic level and concludes, as I did above, that declining search intensity of the long-term unemployed can amount only to a very small effect overall, simply because the long-term unemployed constitute such a small percentage of the total unemployed.

CHAPTER FIVE

1 Broersma and Franses (1994) study an error-correction model for Canadian quarterly unemployment, focusing on whether the model is best estimated with seasonally adjusted or unadjusted data. They find that the seasonal component is predictable within sample, though they do not allow the seasonal component to vary with the state of the economy (so that a firm might hire in the spring, if it hires at all). Also, they do not control for UI and other important changes in the Canadian economy during the period 1964:Q1–1991:Q4 under study.

2 See, for example, Campbell and Perron (1991) and Cochrane's comments (1991) for one overview.

3 The lag operator L maps a variable into its own lagged value, so that $LX_t \equiv X_{t-1}$.

4 Hamilton (1994, 448–9), for example, establishes that the impulse-response coefficients from an ARFIMA model decay more slowly than those of an ARMA model.

5 Koustas and Veloce also report US results using analogous ARFIMA procedures, finding less evidence of persistence than in the Canadian results: US real GDP per capita has an estimated value of d of 0.68, for example. This difference contrasts with Fortin (1993), another recent paper that compares these two countries (but using estimated Phillips curves); in Fortin's account, Canada and the United States appeared to exhibit similar behaviour.

6 For real GDP per capita, the ARFIMA model is $d = 0.9$, $p = 3$, and $q = 3$, where p and q are the orders of the autoregressive and moving-average-lag polynomials, respectively. For unemployment, the model has $(d, p, q) = (0.9, 0, 3)$ and is estimated with allowance for seasonality (Koustas and Veloce 1993, Table 2, p. 12).

7 As Diebold and Rudebusch concluded their influential US study, "However, and most importantly, we argue that the confidence intervals associated with any univariate persistence estimates are likely to be quite wide ... The confidence we can place in *any* estimate of the long-run response is low because there are so few independent observations on long-run behavior available in the data" (1989, 206–7).

8 This framework hence involves testing the alternative of hysteresis against the null of an unchanging natural rate. It is important to realize that a potential rejection of the alternative says little about the validity of the null.

9 As noted above, the output loss is "temporary" in a flow sense, but the stock of output aggregated over time is permanently lower as a result.

10 A more general model would have the change in inflation affected by the level of unemployment and a set of forcing variables F, with arbitrary polynomials in the lag operator on both the change-in-inflation and the unemployment variable. That is, $a(L)(1 - L)\Pi + b(L)U = F$, in which case the sacrifice ratio would be given by $a(1)/b(1)$, the ratio of the leading terms in the $a(L)$ and $b(L)$ polynomials. I thank a referee for this observation.

11 Scarth (1994, 114), in his discussion of Fortin (1994), observes that the standard measure of the sacrifice ratio, $1/(b(1 - h))$ in the present notation, is strongly non-linear in the hysteresis parameter h. For $b = 0.25$, for example, the sacrifice ratio will be 16 if $h = 0.75$ but only 6.4 if $h = 0.375$ (and 4.0 if $h = 0$). He concludes that the quantitative importance of hysteresis really begins to bite only as the parameter h approaches one.

12 Note that neither specification really captures the idea of policy credibility in a fully satisfactory manner. Neither model, for example,

would suggest any change if the bank's policy of low- or zero-inflation targets rapidly became less credible, as might result from, say, a change of governor. To the extent that these ideas are important, this inability to incorporate credibility is a failing of current econometric-modelling capabilities.

13 One difference between these results and those reported in Poloz and Wilkinson (1992), discussed at greater length below, is that I find some evidence of hysteresis in an annualized version of Cozier and Wilkinson's model, while in Poloz and Wilkinson's Table 4 (1992, 130), they do not. The origin of this apparent discrepancy is that, in my analysis, I have entered the unemployment measure contemporaneously and lagged one year, while in their annualization, only the contemporaneous measure is employed.

14 In unpublished comments on an earlier version of this monograph, Pierre Fortin has pointed out that, if one confidently believes that the specification that one has estimated is correct, changes such as removal of some lagged values would introduce a specification error and lead to biased estimates – "hysteresis is forced out, not tested," as he nicely put it. My response is simply that I do not have this degree of confidence in any particular specification. Unless the researcher can construct an adequate theoretical and empirical reason to adopt one exact specification over others that seem "close" in some reasonable sense, I think it quite appropriate to query whether results are particularly sensitive to such small specification changes. Moreover, if such sensitivity is detected, it seems right to think about whether there are theoretical mechanisms that could lead to such apparent singularities in the results. I return to this point, in the context of Tables 5.3 and 5.4, below.

15 This expression comes from evaluation of a quadratic form in the vector of partial derivatives of h with respect to C and L where the weighting matrix has the variances of L and C on the diagonal and their covariance on the off-diagonal.

16 This comment also applies to my annual version of Cozier and Wilkinson's results where some evidence was found supportive of hysteresis.

17 Their adjustment is based on fixed population weights.

18 Of course, this may not be entirely appropriate if it is thought that total unemployment, adult-female unemployment, and youth unemployment are not time-invariant measures of tightness in the labour market as a whole.

CHAPTER SIX

1 This is of course an empirical question, depending as it must on the number of unemployment spells that do in fact end in withdrawal from the labour force, and Jones and Riddell (1995) simulate a number of model economies, parameterized to accord in aggregate with what we know about the Canadian economy, before concluding that the filter problem appears to be severe. However, simulation is not the same as having genuine spell data, and the extent of the LMAS filter must remain unproven.

2 See, for example, Beach and Kaliski (1983) and Hasan and de Broucker (1982) for earlier Canadian work with such data.

3 A description of the LFS survey design may be found in Statistics Canada (1976) and, for changes implemented in 1985, in Statistics Canada (1984). Gross-flow data supplied by Statistics Canada are not available for the periods 1984:10–1985:3 and 1989:12–1990:3.

4 Extensive discussion of these problems and potential methods of correction can be found in Macredie (1983), Abowd and Zellner (1985), Poterba & Summers (1986), Meyer (1988), and Stasny (1988). Some suggestion that these methods of correction may in fact overcorrect is contained in an unpublished paper by LeMaître (n.d.), where it is argued, based on Canadian data, that serial independence of classification errors may be a bad assumption.

5 The LMAS's fourth labour-market state was one of marginal attachment to the labour force, determined by a person's wanting work but not currently seeking it.

6 Ferrall (1994), for example, uses the LMAS in such a two-state world.

7 This is subject to the usual problems of measurement error and so on.

8 Surveys of this duration-modelling approach include Kalbfleisch and Prentice (1980), Cox and Oakes (1984), Kiefer (1988), and Lancaster (1990).

9 There are 797 second spells (ranging from 1 to 3 months) and 12 third spells (necessarily all 1 month long and right-censored).

10 This is a somewhat unusual result in this literature and may suggest that the Weibull specification is incorrect, however.

11 These results contrast to some degree with those of Corak (1990), who studies parametric models of duration using data from the Canadian Annual Work Patterns Survey for 1978–80 and 1982–85, each year being analysed separately. The main thrust of those results was that, while sensitive to the point in the business cycle at

which the data were collected, the conclusions on duration dependence were fairly robust to alternative assumptions as to functional form for the distribution of spells. See also Corak (1993b).

12 The raw data on multiple non-employment spells show 8,757 second spells (44 per cent of which are right-censored), 2,833 third spells (40 per cent right-censored), 1,090 fourth spells (41 per cent right-censored), and smaller numbers of subsequent spells, up to 34 seventh spells of non-employment.

13 The Weibull case without such heterogeneity would result if $1/k$ (which is the variance of ν) were zero.

14 On the dating of the first two recessions, see P. Cross (1988).

15 On its properties and its relation to the new index, see Haggar-Guenette (1988).

16 As noted above, there are also two short gaps in the gross-flow data, so there are actually 147 usable observations.

17 In essence, this amounts to a deterministic approach to seasonality. The principal alternative would be a stochastic treatment of seasonality; see, for instance, Harvey (1989, 40–3).

18 A positive shock to hiring could reduce both unemployment and vacancies in the next period, so that the single-equation estimates of the coefficients on (log) unemployment and (log) vacancies would be biased downward. However, the results below seem to suggest that, if this problem is present, it is not well corrected by the available instruments.

19 Storer (1992, chaps. 2 and 3) examines the regional breakdown of a matching-function approach. See also Storer (1993).

CHAPTER SEVEN

1 Examples of such alternative mechanisms would include lagged duration dependence, other patterns of repeat unemployment spells, and less direct causal mechanisms, perhaps operating through the effect of unemployment on the wages of those employed. Each mechanism could in principle be consistent with the extensive lag structure that appears to be required for the macroeconomic results to display hysteresis.

2 But see Stanton (1988) for doubts about an activist policy stance as a response to hysteresis. McGregor (1988), in a contribution at the same conference, presents the opposite case.

3 See also the discussion of the implications of hysteresis in Blinder (1987). McCallum (1987, 426) argues that the relevant issue in a

rules-versus-discretion debate is not hysteresis versus the natural rate, but rather whether the trend rate of growth of output is independent of monetary growth. See also the related discussion in McCallum (1988, 465). Finally, Lindbeck and Snower (1990) give an account of the policy implications that would follow from adoption of their insider-outsider approach, though their analysis remains static and may not capture the full intertemporal nature of membership effects.

4 There may not be a unique value for the sacrifice ratio if the Phillips curve is non-linear or in a number of other plausible cases. None the less, much of the current debate has been set in the context of simple linear models, so I follow this lead in the brief treatment below.

5 On the usual definition, the sacrifice ratio cumulates the undiscounted output losses.

6 Recall, though, Scarth's (1994, 114) point that the numerical value of the sacrifice ratio is non-linear in the hysteresis parameter, becoming very large only for hysteresis effects close to one.

7 In addition to recognizing uncertainty about the sacrifice ratio, given potential output, a full policy evaluation would also consider the effects of different steady-state levels of inflation on potential output itself (through, for example, allocative or efficiency effects of different levels of inflation). See Selody (1990), Novin (1991), and Cozier and Selody (1992), and, for a sceptical view, see Fortin (1993, 4–7). Relatedly, see Ball, Mankiw, and Romer (1988), who use a nominal-rigidities, "new Keynesian" specification to find that countries with low average inflation have relatively flat short-run Phillips curves, while countries with higher average inflation have steeper short-run tradeoffs.

8 Brainard (1967) remains the classic work in this area, showing that when the parameters of a macroeconomic model are uncertain, an optimal policy amounts to a variance-minimizing portfolio. Durlauf (1989, 110–15) extends this logic to the case of uncertainty about macroeconomic regimes, some of which may have unit roots and some of which do not. He argues that analogous logic will impart a bias toward activism, particularly expansionary policy, as a consequence of the potential gains that could accrue if the non-stationary regime is in fact the relevant one. Sims (1989), however, offers a more sceptical interpretation both of the econometric assessment of non-stationarity and of the policy lessons that might follow from such a finding.

References

Abowd, John M., and Zellner, Arnold. 1985. "Estimating Gross Labour-Force Flows," *Journal of Business and Economic Statistics*, 3, 254–83.

Abraham, Katharine G., and Farber, Henry S. 1987. "Job Duration, Seniority, and Earnings," *American Economic Review* 77, 278–97.

Adams, Charles. 1988. "Hysteresis Effects and Unemployment," in R. Cross, ed., *Unemployment, Hysteresis and the Natural Rate Hypothesis*, Oxford and New York: Basil Blackwell, 392–6.

Albrecht, James W., and Axell, Bo. 1984. "An Equilibrium Model of Search Unemployment," *Journal of Political Economy*, 92, 824–40.

Alogoskoufis, George S., and Manning, Alan. 1988a. "On the Persistence of Unemployment," *Economic Policy*, 3, 428–69.

– 1988b. "Wage Setting and Unemployment Persistence in Europe, Japan and the U.S.A.," *European Economic Review*, 32, 698–706.

Altonji, Joseph C., and Shakotko, Robert A. 1987. "Do Wages Rise with Job Seniority?" *Review of Economic Studies*, 54, 437–59.

Arestis, Philip, and Skott, Peter. 1993. "Conflict, Wage Determination, and Hysteresis in U.K. Wage Determination," *Journal of Post Keynesian Economics*, 15, 365–86.

Ashenfelter, Orley, and Card, David. 1986. "Why Have Unemployment Rates in Canada and the United States Diverged?" *Economica*, 53, S171–S195.

Atkins, Frank, Bruce, Christopher, and King, Ian. 1991. "The Canadian Real Wage Phillips Curve: A Sectoral Shift Interpretation," University of Calgary, Department of Economics Discussion Paper No. 132, May.

Ball, Laurence. 1989. "A Model of Unemployment Persistence," Princeton University, Princeton, NJ, mimeo.

– 1990. "Insiders and Outsiders: A Review Essay," *Journal of Monetary Economics*, 26, 459–69.

– 1993. "What Determines the Sacrifice Ratio?" Princeton University, Princeton, NJ, Working Paper No. 93-21.

– 1994. "Credible Disinflation with Staggered Price-Setting," *American Economic Review*, 84, 282–9.

Ball, Laurence, Mankiw, N. Gregory, and Romer, David. 1988. "The New Keynesian Economics and the Output-Inflation Trade-off," *Brookings Papers on Economic Activity*, 1–65.

Barnes, Ruth, and Picard, André. "Claims Received – a Leading Indicator?" in *Unemployment Insurance Statistics*, Annual Supplement to Statistics Canada Catalogue 73-001 (monthly), Statistics Canada Labour Division, UI Statistics Section, Catalogue 73-2025, pp. 11–16.

Barro, Robert J. 1988. "The Persistence of Unemployment," *American Economic Review (Papers and Proceedings)*, 78, 32–7.

Beach, Charles M., and Kaliski, Stephan F. 1983. "Measuring the Duration of Unemployment from Gross Flow Data," *Canadian Journal of Economics*, 16, 258–63.

Beaudry, Paul, and Koop, Gary. 1993. "Do Recessions Permanently Change Output?" *Journal of Monetary Economics*, 31, 149–63.

Belzil, Christian. 1990. "A Duration Model of Unemployment and Job Search Outcomes," Concordia University, Montreal, Department of Economics Working Paper No. 1990-11, June.

Benhabib, Jess, ed. 1992. *Cycles and Chaos in Economic Equilibrium*, Princeton, NJ: Princeton University Press.

Bertola, Giuseppe. 1990. "Job Security, Employment and Wages," *European Economic Review*, 34, 851–79.

Blanchard, Olivier J. 1981. "What Is Left of the Multiplier-Accelerator?" *American Economic Review (Papers and Proceedings)*, 71, 150–4.

– 1990. "Unemployment: Getting the Questions Right – and Some of the Answers," in J.H. Drèze and C.R. Bean, eds., *Europe's Unemployment Problem*, Cambridge, Mass.: MIT Press, 66–89.

– 1991. "Wage Bargaining and Unemployment Persistence," *Journal of Money, Credit, and Banking*, 23, 277–92.

Blanchard, Olivier J., and Diamond, Peter. 1989. "The Beveridge Curve," *Brookings Papers on Economic Activity*, no. 1, 1–60.

– 1990a. "The Aggregate Matching Function," in P. Diamond, ed., *Growth/Productivity/Unemployment: Essays to Celebrate Bob Solow's Birthday*, Cambridge, Mass.: MIT Press, 159–201.

– 1990b. "The Cyclical Behavior of the Gross Flows of U.S. Workers," *Brookings Papers on Economic Activity*, no. 2, 85–143.

– 1994. "Ranking, Unemployment Duration, and Wages," *Review of Economic Studies*, 61, 417–34.

Blanchard, Olivier J., and Fischer, Stanley. 1989. *Lectures on Macroeconomics*, Cambridge, Mass.: MIT Press.

Blanchard, Olivier J., and Quah, Danny. 1989. "The Dynamic Effects of Aggregate Demand and Supply Disturbances," *American Economic Review*, 79, 655–73.

Blanchard, Olivier J., and Summers, Lawrence H. 1986. "Hysteresis and the European Unemployment Problem," in S. Fischer, ed., *NBER Macroeconomics Annual*, Cambridge, Mass.: MIT Press, 15–78.

– 1987a. "Fiscal Increasing Returns, Hysteresis, Real Wages and Unemployment," *European Economic Review*, 31, 543–66.

– 1987b. "Hysteresis in Unemployment," *European Economic Review*, 31, 288–95.

– 1988. "Beyond the Natural Rate Hypothesis," *American Economic Review (Papers and Proceedings)*, 78, 182–7.

Blank, Rebecca, and Card, David. 1991. "Recent Trends in Insured and Uninsured Unemployment: Is There an Explanation?" *Quarterly Journal of Economics*, 106, 1157–89.

Blinder, Alan S. 1987. "The Rules-versus-Discretion Debate in the Light of Recent Experience," *Weltwirtschaftliches Archiv*, 123, 399–414.

Bliss, Christopher. 1990. "The Natural Rate of Unemployment in a Model with Trade Unions," Nuffield College, Oxford, Discussion Paper No. 54, September.

Brainard, W.C. 1967. "Uncertainty and the Effectiveness of Policy," *American Economic Review (Papers and Proceedings)*, 57, 411–25.

Broersma, Lourens, and Franses, Philip Hans. 1994. "Modeling Quarterly Unemployment in Canada," Erasmus University, Rotterdam, Econometric Institute, mimeo.

Brown, James N. 1989. "Why Do Wages Increase with Tenure? On-the-job Training and Life-Cycle Wage Growth Observed Within Firms," *American Economic Review*, 79, 971–91.

Brown, James N., and Ashenfelter, Orley. 1986. "Testing the Efficiency of Employment Contracts," *Journal of Political Economy*, 94, special issue, S40–S87.

Brunello, Giorgio. 1990. "Hysteresis and 'The Japanese Unemployment Problem': A Preliminary Investigation," *Oxford Economic Papers*, 42, 483–500.

Bruno, Michael, and Sachs, Jeffrey D. 1985. *Economics of Worldwide Stagflation*, Oxford and New York: Basil Blackwell.

Budd, Alan, Levine, Paul, and Smith, Peter. 1988. "Real Wage Adjustment and Long-term Unemployment," in R. Cross, ed., *Unemployment, Hysteresis and the Natural Rate Hypothesis*, Oxford and New York: Basil Blackwell, 41–64.

Burda, Michael C. 1990. "Some Evidence on the Membership Hysteresis Hypothesis in Europe," in Wolfgang Franz, ed., *Hysteresis Effects in Economic Models: Studies in Empirical Economics*, New York: Springer, 35–53.

Burda, Michael, and Wyplosz, Charles. 1990. "Gross Labour Market Flows in Europe: Some Stylized Facts," Centre for Economic Policy Research, London, England, Discussion Paper No. 439, August.

Burns, Andrew. 1990. "Unemployment in Canada, Frictional, Structural and Cyclical Aspects," Ottawa, Economic Council of Canada, Working Paper No. 1.

– 1991a. "The Natural Rate of Unemployment: Canada and the Provinces," in S. Gera, ed., *Canadian Unemployment: Lessons from the 80s and Challenges for the 90s*, Ottawa: Economic Council of Canada, 39–52.

– 1991b. "Regional Unemployment Disparity and Economic Structure," in S. Gera, ed., *Canadian Unemployment: Lessons from the 80s and Challenges for the 90s*, Ottawa: Economic Council of Canada, 79–86.

Campbell, John Y., and Mankiw, N. Gregory. 1987. "Permanent and Transitory Components in Macroeconomic Fluctuations," *American Economic Review (Papers and Proceedings)*, 77, 111–17.

Campbell, John Y., and Perron, Pierre. 1991. "Pitfalls and Opportunities: What Macroeconomists Should Know about Unit Roots," in Olivier Jean Blanchard and Stanley Fischer, eds., *NBER Macroeconomics Annual*, Cambridge, Mass.: MIT Press.

Card, David, and Riddell, W. Craig. 1993. "A Comparative Analysis of Unemployment in Canada and the United States," in David Card and Richard B. Freeman, eds., *Small Differences that Matter: Labor Markets and Income Maintenance in Canada and the United States*, Chicago: University of Chicago Press and NBER, 149–89.

Carmichael, H. Lorne. 1990. "Efficiency Wage Models of Unemployment – One View," *Economic Inquiry*, 28, 269–95.

Carruth, Alan A., and Oswald, Andrew J. 1988. "Testing for Multiple Natural Rates of Unemployment in the British Economy: A Preliminary Investigation," in R. Cross, ed., *Unemployment, Hysteresis and the Natural Rate Hypothesis*, Oxford and New York: Basil Blackwell, 232–55.

Christiano, Lawrence J., and Eichenbaum, Martin. 1990. "Unit Roots in Real GNP: Do We Know, and Do We Care?" *Carnegie-Rochester Conference Series on Public Policy*, 32, 7–71.

Cochrane, John H. 1988. "How Big Is the Random Walk in GNP?" *Journal of Political Economy*, 96, 893–920.

– 1991. "Comment on Campbell and Perron," in Olivier Jean Blanchard and Stanley Fischer, eds., *NBER Macroeconomics Annual*, Cambridge, Mass.: MIT Press, 201–10.

Coe, David T. 1988. "Hysteresis Effects in Aggregate Wage Equations," in R. Cross, ed., *Unemployment, Hysteresis and the Natural Rate Hypothesis*, Oxford and New York: Basil Blackwell, 284–305.

– 1990. "Insider-Outsider Influences on Industry Wages: Evidence from Fourteen Industrialized Countries," in Wolfgang Franz, ed., *Hysteresis Effects in Economic Models: Studies in Empirical Economics*, New York: Springer, 55–75.

Corak, Miles. 1990. "The Duration of Unemployment and the Dynamics of Labour Sector Adjustment: Parametric Evidence from the Canadian Annual Work Patterns Survey, 1978–80, 1982–85," Economic Council of Canada, Ottawa, Working Paper No. 3.

– 1991a. "Canadian Unemployment in Retrospect," in S. Gera, ed., *Canadian Unemployment: Lessons from the 80s and Challenges for the 90s*, Ottawa: Economic Council of Canada, 65–78.

– 1991b. "Traps and Vicious Circles: A Longitudinal Analysis of Participation in the Canadian Unemployment Insurance Program," Statistics Canada, Ottawa, Business and Labour Market Analysis Group, mimeo, November.

– 1991c. "Unemployment Comes of Age: The Demographics of Labour Sector Adjustment in Canada," in S. Gera, ed., *Canadian Unemployment: Lessons from the 80s and Challenges for the 90s*, Ottawa: Economic Council of Canada, 89–98.

– 1992. "Repeat Users of the Unemployment Insurance Program," *Canadian Economic Observer*, Statistics Canada Catalogue 11-010, January, 3.1–3.25.

– 1993a. "Is Unemployment Insurance Addictive? Evidence from the Benefit Durations of Repeat Users," *Industrial and Labor Relations Review*, 47, 62–72.

– 1993b. "The Duration of Unemployment during Boom and Bust," *Canadian Economic Observer*, September, 4.1–4.20.
– 1993c. "Unemployment Insurance Once Again: The Incidence of Repeat Participation in the Canadian UI Program," *Canadian Public Policy*, 19, 162–76.
– 1994a. "Unemployment Insurance, Temporary Layoffs, and Recall Expectations," *Canadian Economic Observer*, May, 3.1–3.15.
– 1994b. "Unemployment Insurance, Work Disincentives, and the Canadian Labor Market: An Overview," in Christopher Green, Fred Lazar, Miles Corak, and Dominique Gross, *Unemployment Insurance: How to Make It Work*, vol. 2 of *The Social Policy Challenge*, Toronto: C.D. Howe Institute, 86–159.
Corak, Miles, and Jones, Stephen R.G. 1993. "The Persistence of Unemployment: How Important Were Regional Extended Unemployment Insurance Benefits?" Statistics Canada, Analytical Studies Branch, Research Paper No. 53. *Canadian Journal of Economics*, forthcoming.
Cox, David R. 1972. "Regression Models and Life-Tables (with Discussion)," *Journal of the Royal Statistical Society*, Series B, 34, 187–220.
Cox, David R., and Oakes, David. 1984. *Analysis of Survival Data*, London: Chapman and Hall.
Cozier, Barry, and Selody, Jack. 1992. "Inflation and Macroeconomic Performance: Some Cross-Country Evidence," Bank of Canada, Ottawa, Working Paper No. 92-6, November.
Cozier, Barry, and Wilkinson, Gordon. 1990. "How Large Are the Costs of Disinflation in Canada?" Bank of Canada, Ottawa, Working Paper No. 90-6.
– 1991. "Some Evidence on Hysteresis and the Costs of Disinflation in Canada," Bank of Canada, Ottawa, Technical Report No. 55.
Cross, P. 1988. "The Current Expansion in an Historical Context," *Canadian Economic Observer*, Statistics Canada Catalogue 11-010, October, 3.1–3.5.
Cross, Rod, ed. 1988. *Unemployment, Hysteresis and the Natural Rate Hypothesis*, Oxford and New York: Basil Blackwell.
Cross, Rod. 1990a. "Hysteresis and Instability in the Natural Rate of Unemployment," in John C. Wood and Ronald N. Woods, eds., *Milton Friedman: Critical Assessments*, London and New York: Routledge, 358–75.
– 1990b. "Phelps, Hysteresis, and the Natural Rate of Unemployment," in John C. Wood and Ronald N. Woods, eds., *Milton Friedman: Critical Assessments*, London and New York: Routledge, 292–8.

– 1993a. "Hysteresis and Post Keynesian Economics," *Journal of Post Keynesian Economics*, 15, 305–8.

– 1993b. "On the Foundations of Hysteresis in Economic Systems," *Economics and Philosophy*, spring, 53–74.

Cross, Rod, and Allan, Andrew. 1988. "On the History of Hysteresis," in R. Cross, ed., *Unemployment, Hysteresis and the Natural Rate Hypothesis*, Oxford and New York: Basil Blackwell, 26–38.

Cross, Rod, and Hutchinson, Harold. 1988. "Hysteresis Effects and Unemployment: An Outline," in R. Cross, ed., *Unemployment, Hysteresis and the Natural Rate Hypothesis*, Oxford and New York: Basil Blackwell, 3–7.

Cross, Rod, Hutchinson, Harold, and Yeoward, Serena. 1990a. "The Natural Rate Hypothesis versus the Hysteresis Hypothesis: A Century of Prices and Unemployment in the U.S. and the U.K.," *Weltwirtschaftliches Archiv*, 126, 156–64.

– 1990b. "The Natural Rate, Hysteresis, and the Duration Composition of Unemployment in the U.S." *Quarterly Journal of Business and Economics*, 29, 89–116.

Crow, John. 1988. "The Work of Monetary Policy (Eric J. Hanson Memorial Lecture delivered at the University of Alberta, Edmonton, Alberta, 18 January 1988)," *Bank of Canada Review*, February, 3–17.

– 1992. "What to Do about the Bank of Canada (Luncheon Remarks to the Canadian Economics Association Annual Meeting, Charlottetown, PEI, 6 June 1992)," *Bank of Canada Review*, June, 3–10.

Dagsvik, John, and Jovanovic, Boyan. 1991. "Was the Great Depression a Low-Level Equilibrium?" New York University, C.V. Starr Center for Applied Economics, Research Report No. 91-07, January.

Darity, William, Jr., and Goldsmith, Arthur H. 1993. "Unemployment, Social Psychology, and Unemployment Hysteresis," *Journal of Post Keynesian Economics*, 16, 55–71.

Davidson, Paul. 1991. "Is Probability Theory Relevant for Uncertainty? A Post Keynesian Perspective," *Journal of Economic Perspectives*, 5, 129–43.

– 1993. "The Elephant and the Butterfly, or Hysteresis and Post Keynesian Economics," *Journal of Post Keynesian Economics*, 15, 309–22.

Day, Richard. 1982. "Irregular Growth Cycles," *American Economic Review*, 72, 406–14.

– 1983. "The Emergence of Chaos from Classical Economic Growth," *Quarterly Journal of Economics*, 98, 201–13.

De Long, J. Bradford, and Summers, Lawrence H. 1988. "How Does Macroeconomic Policy Affect Output?" *Brookings Papers on Economic Activity*, 433–94.

Devereaux, Mary Sue. 1992. "Alternative Measures of Unemployment," *Perspectives on Labour and Income*, winter, 35–43.

Diamond, Peter. 1971. "A Model of Price Adjustment," *Journal of Economic Theory*, 3, 156–68.

– 1982. "Aggregate Demand Management in Search Equilibrium," *Journal of Political Economy*, 90, 881–94.

Dickens, William T. 1982. "The Productivity Crisis," *Economics Letters*, 9, 37–42.

Diebold, F.X., and Rudebusch, G.D. 1989. "Long Memory and Persistence in Aggregate Output," *Journal of Monetary Economics*, 24, 189–209.

Dixit, Avinash. 1989. "Hysteresis, Import Penetration, and Exchange Rate Pass-through," *Quarterly Journal of Economics*, 104, 205–28.

– 1992. "Investment and Hysteresis," *Journal of Economic Perspectives* 6, 107–32.

Dixon, Huw. 1988. "Unions, Oligopoly and the Natural Range of Employment," *Economic Journal*, 98, 1127–47.

Doeringer, Peter, and Piore, Michael. 1971. *Internal Labor Markets and Manpower Analysis*, Lexington, Mass.: Heath.

Drazen, Allan. 1979. "On Permanent Effects of Transitory Phenomena in a Simple Growth Model," *Economics Letters*, 3, 25–30.

– 1985a. "Cyclical Determinants of the Natural Level of Economic Activity," *International Economic Review*, 26, 387–97.

– 1985b. "State Dependence in Optimal Factor Accumulation," *Quarterly Journal of Economics*, 100, 357–72.

Drazen, Allan, and Gottfries, Nils. 1987. "Seniority Rules and the Persistence of Unemployment in a Dynamic Optimizing Model," Institute for International Economic Studies, Stockholm, Seminar Paper No. 387.

Drèze, Jacques H., and Bean, Charles R., eds. 1990. *Europe's Unemployment Problem*, Cambridge, Mass.: MIT Press.

Ducharme, Sophie, Felteau, Claude, and Roy, Paul-Martel. 1992. "Les Déterminants de la durée du chômage dans la région du sud-est de Montréal," Université du Québec à Montréal, Centre de recherche sur les politiques économiques, Cahier de recherche no 84, June.

Durlauf, Steven N. 1989. "Output Persistence, Economic Structure, and the Choice of Stabilization Policy," *Brookings Papers on Economic Activity*, no. 2, 69–136.

– 1991a. "Multiple Equilibria and Persistence in Aggregate Fluctuations," *American Economic Review, Papers and Proceedings*, 81, 70–4.

– 1991b. "Path Dependence in Aggregate Output," Stanford Institute for Theoretical Economics, Technical Report No. 8, May.

– 1993. "Nonergodic Economic Growth," *Review of Economic Studies*, 60, 349–66.

Economic Council of Canada. 1990. *Good Jobs, Bad Jobs: Employment in the Service Economy*, Ottawa: Supply and Services Canada.

Ellis, Christopher J., and Holden, Steinar. 1991. "Hysteresis and the Seniority-Wage Relationship," University of Oslo, Department of Economics, Memorandum No. 9, November.

Ellwood, David T., 1982. "Teenage Unemployment: Permanent Scars or Temporary Blemishes?" in Richard B. Freeman and David Wise, eds., *The Youth Labor Market Problem: Its Nature, Causes, and Consequences*, Chicago: NBER and University of Chicago Press, 349–85.

Espinoza, Maria Paz, and Rhee, Changyong. 1989. "Efficient Wage Bargaining as a Repeated Game," *Quarterly Journal of Economics*, 104, 565–88.

Ewing, James Alfred. 1881. "On the Production of Transient Electric Currents in Iron and Steel Conductors by Twisting Them When Magnetised or by Magnetising Them When Twisted," *Proceedings of the Royal Society of London*, 33, 21–3.

Ferrall, Christopher. 1994. "Unemployment Insurance and Youth Labor Market Behavior in Canada and the United States," Queen's University, Kingston, Ontario, Institute for Economic Research, Discussion Paper No. 904, July.

Flateau, Paul, Lewis, Philip E.T., and Rushton, Allison. 1991. "The Macroeconomic Consequences of Long-term Unemployment," *Australian Economic Review*, 96, 48–56.

Ford, Robert, and Rose, David. 1989. "Estimates of the NAIRU Using an Extended Okun's Law," Bank of Canada, Ottawa, Working Paper No. 89-3.

Fortin, Pierre. 1988. "La Persistance du chômage: synthèse," *L'Actualité économique*, 64, 545–58.

– 1989. "How 'Natural' Is Canada's High Unemployment Rate?" *European Economic Review*, 33, 89–110.

– 1990. "Can the Costs of an Anti-inflation Policy be Reduced?" in Robert C. York, ed., *Taking Aim: The Debate on Zero Inflation*, Toronto: C.D. Howe Institute, 135–67.

– 1991. "The Phillips Curve, Macroeconomic Policy, and the Welfare of Canadians," *Canadian Journal of Economics*, 24, 774–803.

– 1993. "The Unbearable Lightness of Zero-inflation Optimism," *Canadian Business Economics*, spring, 3–18.

– 1994. "Slow Growth, Unemployment and Debt: What Happened? What Can We Do?" in Thomas J. Courchene, ed., *Stabilization, Growth and Distribution: Linkages in the Knowledge Era*, Kingston, Ont.: John Deutsch Institute, 67–108.

Fortin, Pierre, Keil, Manfred, and Symons, James. 1994. "The Sources of Unemployment in Canada, 1963–1991: Evidence from a Panel of Regions and Demographic Groups," Université du Québec à Montréal, miméo.

Fortin, Pierre, and Newton, Keith. 1982. "Labour Market Tightness and Wage Inflation in Canada," in M.N. Baily, ed., *Workers, Jobs, and Inflation*, Washington, DC: Brookings Institution, 243–74.

Fortin, Pierre, and Prévost, Simon. 1993. "Job Search Intensity of the Long-term Unemployed: Evidence from a Panel of Southeast Montreal Workers," Université du Québec à Montréal, Centre de recherche sur l'emploi et les fluctuations économiques, Cahier de recherche no 22, October.

Frank, Jeff. 1990. "Monopolistic Competition, Risk Aversion, and Equilibrium Recessions," *Quarterly Journal of Economics*, 105, 921–38.

Franz, Wolfgang. 1990. "Hysteresis in Economic Relationships: An Overview," in Wolfgang Franz, ed., *Hysteresis Effects in Economic Models: Studies in Empirical Economics*, New York: Springer, 1–17.

Friedman, Milton. 1968. "The Role of Monetary Policy," *American Economic Review*, 58, 1–17.

Fuller, Wayne A. 1976. *Introduction to Statistical Time Series*, New York: Wiley.

Gera, Surendra, ed. 1991. *Canadian Unemployment: Lessons from the 80s and Challenges for the 90s*, Ottawa: Economic Council of Canada.

Gera, Surendra, and McMullen, Kathryn. 1991. "Unemployment in Canada: Issues, Findings, and Implications," in S. Gera, ed., *Canadian Unemployment: Lessons from the 80s and Challenges for the 90s*, Ottawa: Economic Council of Canada, 1–20.

Ghysels, Eric. 1988. "A Study toward a Dynamic Theory of Seasonality for Economic Time Series," *Journal of the American Statistical Association*, 83, 168–72.

– 1990. "Unit Root Tests and the Statistical Pitfalls of Seasonal Adjustment: The Case of U.S. Post-War Real Gross National Product," *Journal of Business and Economic Statistics*, 8, 145–52.

Gordon, Robert J. 1988. "Back to the Future: European Unemployment Today Viewed from America in 1939," *Brookings Papers on Economic Activity*, 271–312.

– 1989. "Hysteresis in History: Was There Ever a Phillips Curve?" *American Economic Review (Papers and Proceedings)*, 79, 220–5.

Gottfries, Nils, and Horn, Henrik. 1987. "Wage Formation and the Persistence of Unemployment," *Economic Journal*, 97, 877–84.

Graafland, J.J. 1991. "On the Causes of Hysteresis in Long-term Unemployment in the Netherlands," *Oxford Bulletin of Economics and Statistics*, 53, 155–70.

Graafland, J.J., and Huizinga, F. 1990. "Age-Related Minimum Wages and Hysteresis in Unemployment," *Economics Letters*, 289–94.

Grandmont, Jean-Michel. 1985. "On Endogenous Competitive Business Cycles," *Econometrica*, 53, 995–1045.

– 1989. "Keynesian Issues and Economic Theory," *Scandinavian Journal of Economics*, 91, 265–93.

Granger, C.W.J., and Joyeux, R. 1980. "An Introduction to Long-memory Time Series Models and Fractional Differencing," *Journal of Time Series Analysis*, 1, 15–29.

Green, David A., and Riddell, W. Craig. 1993a. "The Economic Effects of Unemployment Insurance in Canada: An Empirical Analysis of Disentitlement," *Journal of Labor Economics*, 11 no. 1 (part 2), S96–S147.

– 1993b. "Qualifying for Unemployment Insurance: An Empirical Analysis," University of British Columbia, Vancouver, Department of Economics Discussion Paper No. 93-33, September.

Gregory, R.G. 1986. "Wages Policy and Unemployment in Australia," *Economica*, supplement, 53, S53–S74.

Gross, Dominique M. N.d. "In and Out of Unemployment Insurance in Canada: A Dynamic Approach," Simon Fraser University, Burnaby, BC, Department of Economics, mimeo.

Grossman, Gene M. 1983. "Union Wages, Temporary Layoffs, and Seniority," *American Economic Review*, 73, 277–90.

Grossman, Gene M., and Helpman, Elhanen. 1990. "Hysteresis in the Trade Pattern," Cambridge, Mass., NBER Working Paper No. 3526, December.

Haggar-Guenette, Cynthia. 1988. "The 'Old' and the 'Revised' Help-wanted Index: A Comparison," *Help-wanted Index*, Statistics Canada Catalogue 71-204, last issue (May 1989), 33–5.

Hall, Robert E. 1970. "Why Is the Unemployment Rate So High at Full Employment?" *Brookings Papers on Economic Activity*, no. 3, 369–402.

Ham, John C., and Rea, Samuel A. Jr. 1987. "Unemployment Insurance and Male Unemployment Duration in Canada," *Journal of Labor Economics*, 5, 325–53.

Hamilton, James D. 1994. *Time Series Analysis*, Princeton, NJ: Princeton University Press.

Han, Aaron, and Hausman, Jerry A. 1990. "Flexible Parametric Estimation of Duration and Competing Risk Models," *Journal of Applied Econometrics*, 5, 1–28.

Hargreaves Heap, S.P. 1980. "Choosing the Wrong 'Natural' Rate: Accelerating Inflation or Decelerating Employment and Growth?" *Economic Journal*, 90, 611–20.

Harvey, Andrew C. 1989. *Forecasting, Structural Time Series Models and the Kalman Filter*, Cambridge: Cambridge University Press.

Hasan, A., and de Broucker, P. 1982. "Duration and Concentration of Unemployment," *Canadian Journal of Economics*, 15, 735–56.

Heckman, James J. 1991. "Identifying the Hand of the Past: Distinguishing State Dependence from Heterogeneity," *American Economic Review (Papers and Proceedings)*, 81, 75–9.

Heckman, James J., and Borjas, George J. 1980. "Does Unemployment Cause Future Unemployment? Definitions, Questions, and Answers from a Continuous Time Model of Heterogeneity and State Dependence," *Economica*, 47, 247–83.

Heckman, James J., and Singer, B. 1984. "A Method of Minimizing the Impact of Distributional Assumptions in Econometric Models for Duration Data," *Econometrica*, 52, 271–320.

Heller, Walter P. 1986. "Coordination Failure under Complete Markets with Applications to Effective Demand," in W.P. Heller, R.M. Starr, and D.A. Starrett, eds., *Essays in Honor of Kenneth J. Arrow*, vol. 2, New York: Cambridge University Press., 155–75

Hosking, J.R.M. 1981. "Fractional Differencing," *Biometrica*, 68, 165–76.

Howitt, Peter. 1988. "Business Cycles and Search with Costly Recruiting," *Quarterly Journal of Economics*, 103, 147–65.

– 1990a. "Determinate Outcomes with Multiple Equilibria," University of Western Ontario, London, Ont., mimeo, June.

– 1990b. "Zero Inflation as a Long Term Target," in Richard G. Lipsey, ed., *Zero Inflation: The Goal of Price Stability*, Toronto: C.D. Howe Institute, 67–108.

Howitt, Peter, and McAfee, R. Preston. 1987. "Costly Search and Recruiting," *International Economic Review*, 28, 89–107.

Hughes, Peter R., and Hutchinson, Gillian. 1988. "Unemployment, Irreversibility and the Long-term Unemployed," in R. Cross, ed., *Unemployment, Hysteresis and the Natural Rate Hypothesis*, Oxford and New York: Basil Blackwell, 93–114.

Issac, Alan G. 1993. "Is There a Natural Rate?" *Journal of Post Keynesian Economics*, 15, 453–70.

Jackman, Richard, and Layard, Richard. 1987. "Introduction," *European Economic Review*, 31, 285–7.

– 1991. "Does Long-term Unemployment Reduce a Person's Chance of a Job? A Time-series Test," *Economica*, 58, 93–106.

Jones, Stephen R.G. 1987. "Union Employment and Membership Dynamics," *Economics Letters*, 25, 197–200.

– 1989. "Job Search Methods, Intensity and Effects," *Oxford Bulletin of Economics and Statistics*, 51, 277–96.

– 1993. "Cyclical and Seasonal Properties of Canadian Gross Flows of Labour," *Canadian Public Policy*, 19, 1–17.

Jones, Stephen R.G., and McKenna, C.J. 1989. "The Effect of Outsiders on Union Contracts," *European Economic Review*, 33, 1567–73.

– 1994. "A Dynamic Model of Union Membership and Employment," *Economica*, 61, 179–90.

Jones, Stephen R.G., and Riddell, W. Craig. 1993. "The Measurement of Unemployment: An Empirical Approach," McMaster University, Hamilton, Ont., Department of Economics Working Paper No. 93-12, December.

– 1995. "The Measurement of Labor Market Dynamics with Longitudinal Data: The Labour Market Activity Survey Filter," *Journal of Labor Economics*, 13, 350–84.

Jovanovic, Boyan. 1989. "Observable Implications of Models with Multiple Equilibria," *Econometrica*, 57, 1431–7.

Juhn, C., Murphy, K.M., and Topel, R.H. 1991. "Why Has the Natural Rate of Unemployment Increased over Time?" *Brookings Papers on Economic Activity*, no. 2, 75–126.

Kalbfleisch, John D., and Prentice, Robert L. 1980. *The Statistical Analysis of Failure Time Data*, New York: Wiley.

Kaliski, S.F. 1987. "Accounting for Unemployment – a Labour Market Perspective," *Canadian Journal of Economics*, 20, 665–93.

Katz, Lawrence F. 1988. "Some Recent Developments in Labor Economics and Their Implications for Macroeconomics," *Journal of Money, Credit, and Banking*, 20, 507–30.

Katzner, Donald W. 1993. "Some Notes on the Role of History and the Definition of Hysteresis and Related Concepts in Economic Analysis," *Journal of Post Keynesian Economics*, 15, 323–45.

Keil, M., and Symons, J. 1991. "An Aggregate Model of the Canadian Labour Market," London School of Economics, Centre for Economic Performance, Discussion Paper No. 15.

Kennan, John. 1986. "Comment on Blanchard and Summers," in S. Fischer, ed., *NBER Macroeconomics Annual*, Cambridge, Mass.: MIT Press, 78–84.

– 1988. "Equilibrium Interpretations of Employment and Real Wage Fluctuations," in S. Fischer, ed., *NBER Macroeconomics Annual*, Cambridge, Mass.: MIT Press, 157–205.

Kiefer, Nicholas M. 1988. "Economic Duration Data and Hazard Functions," *Journal of Economic Literature*, 26, 646–79.

King, Ian P. 1990. "A Natural Rate Model of Frictional and Long-term Unemployment," *Canadian Journal of Economics*, 23, 523–45.

Koustas, Zisimos, and Veloce, William. 1993. "Unemployment Hysteresis in Canada: An Approach Based on Long-memory Time Series Models," Brock University, St Catharines, Ont., Department of Economics, mimeo, June.

Kuhn, Peter, and Robb, A. Leslie. 1994. "Unemployment, Skill and Labour Supply: Evidence from Canadian Microdata, 1971–1991," McMaster University, Hamilton, Ont., mimeo, May.

Laidler, David. 1990. "The Zero-inflation Target," in Richard G. Lipsey, ed., *Zero Inflation: The Goal of Price Stability*, Toronto: C.D. Howe Institute, 131–51.

Lancaster, Tony. 1990. *The Econometric Analysis of Transition Data*, Cambridge: Cambridge University Press.

Lang, Kevin, and Kahn, Shulamit. 1990. "Efficiency Wage Models of Unemployment – a Second View," *Economic Inquiry*, 28, 296–306.

Laxton, Douglas, Rose, David, and Tetlow, Robert. 1993a. "Is the Canadian Phillips Curve Non-linear?" Bank of Canada, Ottawa, Working Paper No. 93-7, July.

– 1993b. "Problems in Identifying Non-linear Phillips Curves: Some Further Consequences of Mismeasuring Potential Output," Bank of Canada, Ottawa, Working Paper No. 93-6, June.

Laxton, Douglas, Shoom, Kevin, and Tetlow, Robert. 1992. "Should the Change in the Gap Appear in the Phillips Curve? Some Consequences of Mismeasuring Potential Output," Bank of Canada, Ottawa, Working Paper No. 92-1, January.

Layard, Richard, and Bean, Charles. 1989. "Why Does Unemployment Persist?" *Scandinavian Journal of Economics*, 91, 371–96.

Layard, Richard, and Nickell, Stephen. 1986. "Unemployment in Britain," *Economica*, 53, supplement, S121–S169.

– 1987. "The Labour Market," in R. Dornbusch and R. Layard, eds., *The Performance of the British Economy*, Oxford: Clarendon Press, 131–79.

– 1991. "Unemployment in the OECD Countries," Oxford University, Applied Economics Discussion Paper No. 130, December.

Layard, Richard, Nickell, Stephen, and Jackman, Richard. 1991. *Unemployment: Macroeconomic Performance and the Labour Market*, Oxford: Oxford University Press.

LeMaître, Georges. N.d. "The Measurement and Analysis of Gross Flows," Statistics Canada, Ottawa, Social Survey Methods Division, mimeo.

Lever, M.C.H. 1991. "Union Wage Setting and Unemployment in the Netherlands (1965–1987)," *Applied Economics*, 23, 1579–85.

Lévesque, Jean-Marc. 1987. "A Comparison of Unemployment Data from Two Sources: The Unemployment Insurance Program and the Labour Force Survey," Statistics Canada, Ottawa, Labour and Household Surveys Analysis Division, Staff Report, April.

– 1989. "Unemployment and Unemployment Insurance: A Tale of Two Sources," *Perspectives on Labour and Income*, winter, 49–57.

Lindbeck, Assar. 1989. "Remaining Puzzles and Neglected Issues in Macroeconomics," *Scandinavian Journal of Economics*, 91, 495–516.

Lindbeck, Assar, and Snower, Dennis. 1988. *The Insider-Outsider Theory of Employment and Unemployment*, Cambridge, Mass.: MIT Press.

– 1990. "Demand- and Supply-side Policies and Unemployment: Policy Implications of the Insider-Outsider Approach," *Scandinavian Journal of Economics*, 92, 279–305.

Lipsett, Brenda, and James, Steven. N.d. "Interpreting Sacrifice Ratios across Countries and over Time: A Cautionary Note," Department of Finance, Ottawa, Economic Studies and Policy Analysis, mimeo.

Lipsey, Richard G., ed. 1990. *Zero Inflation: The Goal of Price Stability*, Toronto: C.D. Howe Institute.

Lucas, Robert E., Jr., and Prescott, Edward. 1974. "Equilibrium Search and Unemployment," *Journal of Economic Theory*, 7, 188–209.

McCallum, Bennett T. 1987. "The Case for Rules in the Conduct of Monetary Policy: A Concrete Example," *Weltwirtschaftliches Archiv*, 123, 415–29.

– 1988. "Postwar Developments in Business Cycle Theory: A Moderately Classical Perspective," *Journal of Money, Credit, and Banking*, 20, 459–71.

– 1989. "New Classical Macroeconomics: A Sympathetic Account," *Scandinavian Journal of Economics*, 91, 223–52.

McCallum, John. 1987. "Unemployment in Canada and the United States," *Canadian Journal of Economics*, 20, 802–22.

– 1988. "Les Taux de chômage canadien et américan dans les années 1980: un test de trois hypothèses," *L'Actualité économique*, 64, 494–508.

MaCurdy, Thomas E., and Pencavel, John H. 1986. "Testing between Competing Models of Wage and Employment Determination in Unionized Markets," *Journal of Political Economy*, 94, special issue, S3–S39.

McDonald, Ian, and Solow, Robert M. 1981. "Wage Bargaining and Employment," *American Economic Review*, 71, 896–908.

– 1985. "Wages and Employment in a Segmented Labor Market," *Quarterly Journal of Economics*, 100, 1115–41.

McGregor, Peter G. 1988. "Hysteresis and Unemployment Policy: The Case for Activism," in R. Cross, ed., *Unemployment, Hysteresis and the Natural Rate Hypothesis*, Oxford and New York: Basil Blackwell, 402–6.

Macredie, Ian. 1983. "The Impact of Response Errors in the Estimation of Labour Market Flows," Statistics Canada, Ottawa, Economic Characteristics Division, Labour Force Activity Section, mimeo, October.

Malinvaud, E. 1986. "The Rise of Unemployment in France," *Economica*, 53, supplement, S197–S217.

Mankiw, N. Gregory, Romer, David, and Weil, David N. 1992. "A Contribution to the Empirics of Economic Growth," *Quarterly Journal of Economics*, 107, 407–37.

Manning, Alan. 1990. "Imperfect Competition, Multiple Equilibria and Unemployment Policy," *Economic Journal (Conference Papers)*, 100, 151–62.

– 1991. "The Determinants of Wage Pressure: Some Implications of a Dynamic Model," *Economica*, 58, 325–39.

– 1992. "Multiple Equilibria in the British Labour Market: Some Empirical Evidence," *European Economic Review*, 36, 1333–65.

– 1993. "A Dynamic Model of Union Power, Wages and Employment," *Scandinavian Journal of Economics*, 95, 175–93.

Meyer, Bruce D. 1988. "Classification-Error Models and Labor-Market Dynamics," *Journal of Business and Economic Statistics*, 6, 385–90.

– 1990. "Unemployment Insurance and Unemployment Spells," *Econometrica*, 58, 757–82.

Milbourne, Ross D., Purvis, Douglas D., and Scoones, David. 1991. "Unemployment Insurance and Unemployment Dynamics," *Canadian Journal of Economics*, 24, 804–26.

Miller, Marcus H. 1988. "Hysteresis in Output and Employment: A Comment," in R. Cross, ed., *Unemployment, Hysteresis and the Natural Rate Hypothesis*, Oxford and New York: Basil Blackwell, 397–401.

Moffitt, Robert. 1985. "Unemployment Insurance and the Distribution of Unemployment Spells," *Journal of Econometrics*, 28, 85–101.

Möller, J. 1990. "Unemployment and Deterioration of Human Capital," *Empirical Economics*, 15, 199–215.

Moorthy, Vivek. 1990. "Unemployment in Canada and the United States: The Role of Unemployment Insurance Benefits," *Federal Reserve Bank of New York Quarterly*, 14, 48–61.

Mortensen, Dale T. 1989. "The Persistence and Indeterminacy of Unemployment in Search Equilibrium," *Scandinavian Journal of Economics*, 91, 347–70.

– 1991. "Equilibrium Unemployment Cycles," Northwestern University, Evanston, Ill., mimeo, March.

Murphy, Kevin M., and Topel, Robert H. 1987. "The Evolution of Unemployment in the United States: 1968–1985," *NBER Macroeconomics Annual*, 2, 11–58.

Neftçi, S.N. 1984. "Are Economic Time Series Asymmetric over the Business Cycle?" *Journal of Political Economy*, 92, 307–28.

Nelson, Charles R., and Plosser, Charles I. 1982. "Trends and Random Walks in Macroeconomic Time Series," *Journal of Monetary Economics*, 10, 139–62.

Neudorfer, Peter, Pichelmann, Karl, and Wagner, Michael. 1990. "Hysteresis, Nairu and Long Term Unemployment in Austria," in Wolfgang Franz, ed., *Hysteresis Effects in Economic Models: Studies in Empirical Economics*, New York: Springer, 109–21.

Nickell, Stephen, and Kong, Paul. 1992. "An Investigation into the Power of Insiders in Wage Determination," *European Economic Review*, 36, 1573–99.

Nickell, Stephen, and Wadhwani, Sushil. 1990. "Insider Forces and Wage Determination," *Economic Journal*, 100, 496–509.

Novin, Farid. 1991. "The Productivity-Inflation Nexus Revisited: Canada, 1969–1988," Bank of Canada, Ottawa, Working Paper No. 91-1.

Osberg, Lars. 1991. "Unemployment and Inter-industry Labour Mobility in Canada in the 1980s," *Applied Economics*, 23, 1707–17.

– 1993. "Fishing in Different Pools: Job-Search Strategies and Job-Finding Success in Canada in the Early 1980s," *Journal of Labor Economics*, 11, 348–86.

Osberg, Lars, Erksoy, Sadettin, and Phipps, Shelley. 1993. "Unemployment, Unemployment Insurance and the Redistribution of Income in Canada in the 1980s: Provisional Results," Dalhousie University, Halifax, NS, Department of Economics Working Paper No. 93-07, June.

Phaneuf, Louis. 1988. "Hystérésis du chômage: faits, théories et politiques," *L'Actualité économique*, 64, 509–31.

Phelps, Edmund. 1972. *Inflation Policy and Unemployment Theory*, New York: Norton.

– 1979. *Studies in Macroeconomic Theory: Volume 1, Employment and Inflation*, New York: Academic Press.

– 1994. *Structural Slumps: The Modern Equilibrium Theory of Unemployment, Interest, and Assets*, Cambridge, Mass.: Harvard University Press.

Phillips, P.C.B., and Perron, P. 1988. "Testing for a Unit Root in Time Series Regressions," *Biometrica*, 65, 355–46.

Picot, G., LeMaître, G., and Kuhn, P. 1994. "Labour Markets and Layoffs during the Last Two Recessions," *Canadian Economic Observer*, March, 4.1–4.13.

Pissarides, Christopher A. 1986. "Unemployment and Vacancies in Britain," *Economic Policy*, 1, 500–59.

– 1990. *Equilibrium Unemployment Theory*, Oxford and New York: Basil Blackwell.

– 1992. "Loss of Skill during Unemployment and the Persistence of Employment Shocks," *Quarterly Journal of Economics*, 107, 1371–91.

– N.d. "Unemployment Fluctuations with Different Job Durations," London School of Economics and University of California – Berkeley, mimeo.

Poloz, Stephen S., and Wilkinson, Gordon. 1992. "Is Hysteresis a Characteristic of the Canadian Labour Market? A Tale of Two Studies," Bank of Canada, Ottawa, Working Paper No. 92-3, May.

Poterba, James M., and Summers, Lawrence H. 1986. "Reporting Errors and Labor Market Dynamics," *Econometrica*, 54, 1319–38.

Preston, R.S., Saiyed, Haider, and Burns, Andrew. 1992. "The Natural Rate, Scarring, Cycles, Shocks, Persistence and Hysteresis," Economic Council of Canada, Ottawa, mimeo.

Price, Simon. 1992. "Human Capital, Hysteresis and Unemployment among Workers with Finite Lives," *Scottish Journal of Political Economy*, 39, 201–12.

Quah, Danny. 1992. "The Relative Importance of Permanent and Transitory Components: Identification and Some Theoretical Bounds," *Econometrica*, 60, 107–18.

Rahman, Syed S., and Gera, Surendra. 1991. "Long-term Unemployment in Canada: Its Causes and Policy Implications," in S. Gera, ed., *Canadian Unemployment: Lessons from the 80s and Challenges for the 90s*, Ottawa: Economic Council of Canada, 99–116.

Ridder, Geert. 1986. "The Sensitivity of Duration Models to Misspecified Unobserved Heterogeneity and Duration Dependence," University of Amsterdam, mimeo.

Roberts, Kevin. 1989. "The Theory of Union Behaviour: Labour Hoarding and Endogenous Hysteresis," London School of Economics, Discussion Paper No. TE/89/209, October.

Romer, David. 1989. "Comment on Durlauf," *Brookings Papers on Economic Activity*, no. 2, 117–25.

Rose, David E. 1990. "The NAIRU in Canada: Concepts, Determinants and Estimates," Bank of Canada, Ottawa, Technical Report No. 50, December.

Roy, F. 1994. "Unemployment and Unemployment Insurance: An Update," *Canadian Economic Observer*, January, 3.1–3.10.

Salop, Steven C. 1979. "A Model of the Natural Rate of Unemployment," *American Economic Review*, 69, 117–25.

Samson, Lucie. 1988. "Chocs sectoriels et chômage," *L'Actualité économique*, 64, 532–44.

Samuelson, Paul A. 1972. "Some Notions of Causality and Teleology in Economics," in R.C. Merton, ed., *The Collected Scientific Papers of Paul A. Samuelson*, vol. 3, Cambridge, Mass.: MIT Press, 428–72.

Sargent, Thomas. 1983. "Stopping Moderate Inflations: The Methods of Poincaré and Thatcher," in R. Dornbusch and Simonsen, eds., *Inflation, Debt and Indexation*, Cambridge, Mass.: MIT Press, 54–78.

Scarth, William. 1993. "Discussion of 'Trade Hysteresis: Theory and Evidence for Canada' (Robert Amano, Eugene Beaulieu and Lawrence Schembri)," in *The Exchange Rate and the Economy*, Proceedings of a Conference held at the Bank of Canada, Ottawa, 22–23 June 1992, 469–79.

– 1994. "Alternative Assignments of Policy Instruments to Macroeconomic Goals: Comment," in Thomas J. Courchene, ed., *Stabilization,*

Growth and Distribution: Linkages in the Knowledge Era, Kingston, Ont.: John Deutsch Institute, 109–20.

Selody, Jack. 1990. "The Goal of Price Stability: A Review of the Issues," Bank of Canada, Ottawa, Technical Report No. 54.

Setterfield, Mark. 1993. "Towards a Long-run Theory of Effective Demand: Modelling Macroeconomics Systems with Hysteresis," *Journal of Post Keynesian Economics*, 15, 347–64.

Setterfield, M.A., Gordon, D.V., and Osberg, L. 1992. "Searching for a Will o' the Wisp: An Empirical Study of the NAIRU in Canada," *European Economic Review*, 36, 119–36.

Shapiro, Carl, and Stiglitz, Joseph E. 1984. "Equilibrium Unemployment as a Worker Discipline Device," *American Economic Review*, 74, 433–44.

Shapiro, Matthew D., and Watson, Mark W. 1988. "Sources of Business Cycle Fluctuations," in S. Fischer, ed., *NBER Macroeconomics Annual*, Cambridge, Mass.: MIT Press, 111–47.

Sims, Christopher A. 1989. "Comment on Durlauf," *Brookings Papers on Economic Activity*, no. 2, 125–9.

Sneessens, Henri R., and Drèze, Jacques H. 1986. "A Discussion of Belgian Unemployment, Combining Traditional Concepts and Disequilibrium Econometrics," *Economica*, 53, supplement, S89–S119.

Solow, Robert M. 1985. "Insiders and Outsiders in Wage Determination," *Scandinavian Journal of Economics*, 87, 411–28.

Stanton, David. 1988. "Hysteresis: Some Policy Implications," in R. Cross, ed., *Unemployment, Hysteresis and the Natural Rate Hypothesis*, Oxford and New York: Basil Blackwell, 389–91.

Stasny, Elizabeth A. 1988. "Modeling Nonignorable Nonresponse in Categorical Panel Data with an Example in Estimating Gross Labor-Force Flows," *Journal of Business and Economic Statistics*, 6, 207–19.

Statistics Canada. 1976. *Methodology of the Canadian Labour Force Survey*, Ottawa: Statistics Canada.

– 1984. "Post '81 Censal Redesign of the Canadian Labour Force Survey," *Survey Methodology*, Catalogue 12-001, vol. 10, No. 2, December, 127–40.

– 1990. *LMAS Microdata User's Guide: 1986–1987 Longitudinal File*, Ottawa: Statistics Canada.

Stern, Jon. 1986. "Repeat Unemployment Spells: The Effect of Unemployment Benefits on Entry," in Richard Blundell and Ian Walker, eds., *Unemployment, Search and Labour Supply*, Cambridge: Cambridge University Press, 23–43.

Stock, James H. 1987. "Measuring Business Cycle Time," *Journal of Political Economy*, 95, 1240–61.

– 1988. "Estimating Continuous Time Processes Subject to Time Deformation," *Journal of the American Statistical Association*, 83, 77–85.

– 1991. "Hysteresis and the Evolution of Postwar U.S. and U.K. Unemployment," in W. Barnett, J. Geweke, and K. Shell, eds., *Economic Complexity, Chaos, Sunspots, Bubbles, and Nonlinearity: Proceedings of the 4th International Symposium in Economic Theory and Econometrics*, Cambridge: Cambridge University Press, 361–82.

Storer, Paul. 1992. "Multi-sector Labour Market Search: Interactions between Unemployment Duration and Sectoral Shocks," PHD thesis, Department of Economics, University of Western Ontario, London, Ont.

– 1993. "Why Has the Unemployment Rate Become More Persistent in Canada than in the United States?" Université du Québec à Montréal, mimeo, July.

Storer, Paul, and Van Audenrode, Marc A. 1993. "Unemployment Insurance Take-up Rates in Canada: Facts, Determinants, and Implications," Université du Québec à Montréal, mimeo, August.

Sueyoshi, Glenn T. 1992. "Semiparametric Proportional Hazards Estimation of Competing Risks Models with Time-varying Covariates," *Journal of Econometrics*, 51, 25–58.

Summers, Lawrence H. 1988. "Should Keynesian Economics Dispense with the Phillips Curve?" in R. Cross, ed., *Unemployment, Hysteresis and the Natural Rate Hypothesis*, Oxford and New York: Basil Blackwell, 11 25.

Sunter, Deborah. 1994. "Youths – Waiting It Out," *Perspectives on Labour and Income*, spring, 31–6.

Tobin, James. 1972. "Inflation and Unemployment," *American Economic Review*, 62, 1–18.

– 1980. "Stabilization Policy Ten Years After," *Brookings Papers on Economic Activity*, 1, 19–71.

Topel, Robert H. 1991. "Specific Capital, Mobility, and Wages: Wages Rise with Job Seniority," *Journal of Political Economy*, 99, 145–76.

Vendrik, Maarten C.M. 1993. "Habits, Hysteresis and Catastrophes in Labor Supply," *Journal of Economic Behavior and Organization*, 20, 353–72.

Willis, Robert. 1982. "Comment on Ellwood," in Richard B. Freeman and David Wise, eds., *The Youth Labor Market Problem: Its Nature, Causes, and Consequences*, Chicago: NBER and University of Chicago Press, 386–9.

Winter, E.R. 1991. "Some Micro Evidence on Unemployment Persistence," *Oxford Bulletin of Economics and Statistics*, 53, 27–43.

York, Robert C., ed., 1990. *Taking Aim: The Debate on Zero Inflation*, Toronto: C.D. Howe Institute.

Index